Himmler

Israel After Calamity

Israel after Calamity

The Book of Lamentations

Jacob Neusner

The Bible of Judaism Library

Trinity Press International
Valley Forge, Pennsylvania

First Edition 1995

Trinity Press International
P.O. Box 851
Valley Forge, PA 19482-0851

Cover design by Brian Preuss
Cover art: *Purple Current* by Suzanne R. Neusner

Library of Congress Cataloging-in-Publication Data

Neusner, Jacob, 1932–
    Israel after calamity : the Book of Lamentations / Jacob Neusner.
    — 1st ed.
        p.   cm. — (The Bible of Judaism library)
    Includes English translations of selections form Lamentations and the Midrash rabbah on Lamentations.
    Includes bibliographical references and index.
    ISBN 1-56338-105-2
    1. Midrash rabbah. Lamentations—Commentaries. 2. Bible. O.T. Lamentations—Commentaries.   I. Bible. O.T. Lamentations. English. Selections. 1995. II. Midrash rabbah. Lamentations. English. Selections. III. Title. IV. Series.
BM517.M74N49 1995
296.1'4—dc20   95-16096
                                                                                  CIP

Printed in the United States of America

95 96 97 98 99   5 4 3 2 1

Table of Contents

4

Petihta Twenty-Four

The Valley of Vision Pronouncement. What can have happened to you that you have gone, all of you, up on the roofs, O you who were full of tumult, you clamorous town, you city so gay? Your slain are not the slain of the sword, nor the dead of battle. Your officers have all departed; they fled far away; your survivors were all taken captive, taken captive without their bows. That is why I say, "Let me be, I will weep bitterly. Press not to comfort me for the ruin of my poor people."

5

Parashah I

Lamentations 1:3

Judah has gone into exile because of affliction and hard servitude; she dwells now among the nations, but finds no resting place; her pursuers have all overtaken her in the midst of her distress.

6

Parashah I

Lamentations 1:5

Her foes have become the head, her enemies prosper, because the Lord has made her suffer for the multitude of her transgressions; her children have gone away, captives before the foe.

7

Parashah I

Lamentations 1:16

For these things I weep; my eyes flow with tears; for a comforter is far from me, one to revive my courage; my children are desolate, for the enemy has prevailed.

The Bible of Judaism Library Series Foreword

All three heirs to ancient Israel's holy writings, Islam, Christianity, and Judaism, in addition to scripture revere other scriptures or traditions, the New Testament, the corpus of the oral Torah, and the Quran, for Christianity, Judaism, and Islam respectively. All three also maintain that the sense of these subsequent messages from God infuse the original writings, Moses being represented as a rabbi, the prophets as predicting Christ, for the instances of Judaism and Christianity respectively. So the scriptures held in common form a principal arena of confrontation.

But they can also provide the occasion for dialogue, with each biblical religion contributing a sense unique to itself for the illumination of the others' readings of the same writings. And, it is clear, while "Judaism," "Christianity," and "Islam" encompass religious systems of considerable diversity, all Judaisms differ from all Christianities and all Islams in their reading of those scriptures. If we want to understand the religions of monotheism, therefore, we have to grasp how each of them has received and read ancient Israel's scriptures. Comparison begins on the foundations of what is shared, and for Judaism and Christianity the written Torah, or Old Testament, is what is revered in common. And the task of comparison defines the first step toward mutual understanding and respect: here we differ, there we concur, within a single agendum.

Traditions that cannot even agree on the enumeration of the years — whether from the creation of the world, as in Judaism, or from the advent of Christ, as in Christianity, or from the Hegira, as in Islam — can hardly be expected to agree on much else. But, since they do agree on the sacred standing of ancient Israel's scriptures, that is a starting point for conversation in a rational and orderly spirit. For, after all, Judaism, Christianity, and Islam do agree on what is most important of all: that there is one God, creator of heaven and earth, whom alone we worship, by whom alone we are judged, and who has spoken to us uniquely in the scriptures of ancient Israel. We do well, then, to read one another's reading of that common scripture. To that task of forming a spirit of cooperation among the monotheist religions, I dedicate this library of how Judaism reads the ancient Israelite scriptures.

By "Judaism" I mean the Judaism of the dual Torah, oral and written, which conceives that at Mount Sinai God gave to Moses, our rabbi, the Torah, that is, God's will for humanity, exhaustive and whole, in two media, written and oral. The written Torah is found in the Hebrew scriptures that Christianity knows as the Old Testament. The oral Torah was handed on from Moses to Joshua, the prophets, and finally to the sages at the end of a long chain of tradition. The sages produced the writings we now possess under the names of the Mishnah (ca. 200 C.E.), which is amplified in three further writings, the Tosefta (ca. 300), the two Talmuds, the Talmud of the Land of Israel (ca. 400 C.E.) and the Talmud of Babylonia (ca. 600 C.E.). Along with the Mishnah and its expansions in the commentaries of the Tosefta and the two Talmuds, these same sages produced expansions and commentaries on the written Torah, called Midrash compilations, that is, compilations of exegeses of scripture.

The books of the Hebrew scriptures that received such amplifications were those that figured prominently in synagogue liturgy, being read either from week to week, as in the case of the Pentateuch, or Five Books of Moses (Genesis, Exodus, Leviticus, Numbers, Deuteronomy), or on festival occasions in that same liturgical year. Chief among the former are Genesis Rabbah, to Genesis (ca. 450 C.E.); Sifra, to Leviticus (ca. 300); Leviticus Rabbah, also to Leviticus (ca. 450 C.E.); Sifré, to Numbers (ca. 300); Sifré, to Deuteronomy (ca. 300). Addressed to liturgical high points in the year are Pesiqta deRab Kahana (ca. 500 C.E.), which is organized around Sabbaths bearing a particular distinction; and Song of Songs Rabbah, Lamentations Rabbati, Esther Rabbah, and Ruth Rabbah, all of them reaching closure at about the same time as the Talmud of Babylonia, ca. 600. These are read on the occasions of Passover, the ninth of Ab (commemorating the destruction of the Temple in 586 B.C.E., 70 C.E., the expulsion of the Jews from Spain in 1492, and other mournful days), Purim, and Pentecost, respectively.

In the first six titles of this library I set forth a representative sample of the way in which, in its definitive writings, the Judaism of the dual Torah, oral and written, received the Hebrew scriptures and turned all of them into components of its Torah. My goal is that readers find it possible to open the Midrash compilations on their own, guided by the rules of reading set forth here, and find intelligible the modes of reading and writing with scripture in other parts of the compilations I present in these volumes.

Specifically, in these volumes we address exemplary passages of six of the great liturgical responses to scripture: two of the Pentateuchal books, Genesis and Leviticus, and four of the scrolls read on special occasions in the synagogue, Esther, Lamentations, Ruth, and Song of Songs. Upon the classical writings of that Judaism, which took shape in the first seven centuries of the Common Era (C.E. = A.D.), every Judaic system today draws in abundance. Consequently, when we know how the Judaism of the dual Torah read scripture in its formative age, we gain access to the way in which, through the centuries since that time, the Hebrew scriptures entered that dual Torah that formed the theology and law of Judaism. For within Judaism, the name of that Judaism is simply "the Torah," as "the Torah teaches," or "the Torah commands."

What we want to know in these Midrash compilations concerns

the way in which scripture makes its entry into the Torah. That formulation will strike readers as curious, since, after all, everyone knows, scripture (once more: "the Old Testament" or "the written Torah") is the Torah. But that formulation of matters — how scripture enters the Torah — is native to Judaism, since, as we realize, Judaism conceives "the Torah" to encompass tradition in addition to scripture, Torah in an oral as well as in a written medium of formulation and transmission. And, while as a matter of fact the written Torah enjoys a privileged position within the Torah, still it forms only part of the Torah, not the whole of it. Hence it is quite correct to ask how scripture is received within the Torah.

Each of the scriptural books that undergoes the reading of a Midrash compilation yields its own message; none emerges as a mere paraphrase of the plain sense of scripture itself. There was no conception of a historical, limited, particular plain sense, which stood in judgment on fanciful and figurative senses of an other-than-historical, one-time meaning. Hence when our sages read the story of Jacob and Esau as the tale of Israel and Rome in the time of the Christian emperors, as they did, they did not conceive that theirs was a reading distinct from the author's original intention. And how could such a conception have taken root, when, after all, they knew that Torah, oral and written, came from God to Moses, or was the work of the Holy Spirit, or otherwise transcended the particularities of time, space, and circumstance? What today people mean by the "plain" or "original" meaning of scripture, for our sages corresponded to God's intent. And no one, then or now, can imagine that God spoke to only one time or place or circumstance or person. God spoke, everywhere and all the time, eternally, to Israel. And our sages mediated that statement to the Israel of their time and place. The framers of the Midrash compilations wrote through scripture, with scripture, about scripture — and that is how they made their statement of the Torah, oral and written, in a cogent way. That dual mode of discourse — about and through scripture, on the one side, with their own words and through available compositions, on the other side — accounts for the way in which they expressed themselves.

Scripture provided language not only in the concrete sense of verses but in the figurative sense as well. In the latter sense, scripture made available stories, heroes, events, attitudes — the entire repertoire of convention in thought and conviction alike. Writing with scripture meant appealing to the facts that scripture provided to prove propositions that the authorships at hand wished to prove. As a mode of discourse it required forming out of scripture the systems these writers proposed to construct. Accordingly, in dialogue with scripture they made important statements, some of them paraphrases of lessons of scripture, others entirely their own. In the aggregate, our authorship turned to scripture not principally for proof texts, let alone for pretexts, to say whatever they wanted to say anyhow. They read scripture because they wanted to know what it said, but they took for granted that it spoke to them in particular. No other premise of the focus of scriptural discourse was possible; none was ever entertained.

But scripture always remained separate, always marked off. The language of the Hebrew scriptures is different from the language of the Mishnah and Midrash compilations, two varieties of Hebrew. Not only so, but the citation of a verse of scripture very commonly is introduced by "as it is said" or "as it is written" or otherwise distinguished by its position in a larger composition, so that a clear frontier delineates scripture from Midrash. In the language of contemporary literary criticism, the Midrash writings in no way were "intertextual," but all of the writings of the Judaism of the dual Torah other than scripture stood in an intratextual relationship to scripture. So we may say that the founders of Judaism engaged in dialogue with the scriptures of ancient Israel. But it was a dialogue of their own design, on a program of topics of their own concern, for a purpose of their own choosing. Whether or not their statement accorded with the position of scripture on a given point, or merely said the simple and obvious sense of scripture, or found ample support in proof texts — none of these considerations bears material consequence.[1] What matters in the interpretation of the document is the document's own problem: how and why did those who compiled these materials consider that they made a statement, not of their own but of truth? And the answer, as we shall now see, is that they so selected and arranged what they inherited, they so framed and shaped what they themselves made up for their document, as to say in their own words and in scripture's words a single proposition that they — with complete justification — identified with both themselves and with scripture.

The ancient rabbis read scripture as God's personal letter to them. In the rabbis who produced the Midrash compilations laid out in these pages we find an example of how sages, faced with challenge from without and crisis from within, found in scripture the wisdom and the truth that guided them. No wonder, then, that these same figures undertook to answer the letter with a letter of their own. In these books we peer over their shoulders to read the letter they wrote back: their response to God's message to them, this morning, here and now. Here is no work of mere historical interest but a heritage of vital religious faith. For when we encounter how our sages read and answered God's letter to them, those of us who revere scripture as God's word and who open scripture in our quest for God (in the language of Judaism, who come to the Torah to learn God's will) find a model for ourselves.

My goal is to open up for contemporary faith yet another route to Sinai: the one explored by the sages of Judaism — the religion of the dual Torah, written and oral — who received the Torah as God's letter to each of them, personally, this morning. And that response to scripture — God's personal message for today — we share, we who open scripture today, as in ages past and all time to come because it is how and where we find God. If this library succeeds in its mission, faithful Jews and Christians will renew for themselves a program of Bible study, one that brings to scripture profoundly religious concerns in place of the presently prevailing program of historical and philological research. No one dismisses as inconsequential the results of that secular scholarship, for the informed exegesis of words and phrases and sentences of scripture, not to mention the contexts to which those sentences made their statement, draws upon those results. But scholarship does not deliver scripture into our hands, and scholarship does not teach lessons of transcendence, such as the Torah teaches. Scholarship in biblical studies provides inert information; faith makes scripture live and, with it, the results of scholarship too. So let us get our perspective in line with the facts of faith. In this library we see how faithful Judaic sages accomplished that reading, and it was their reading of scripture — and no this-worldly historical, philological reading of scripture — that endowed scripture with sanctity and authority through the ages to our own day.

Note

1. To be sure, these considerations form part of the massive system of theological apologetics created for Judaism in modern times: Judaism, not Christianity, states "the plain meaning of scripture," so that, e.g., Isaiah could not possibly have been referring to Jesus Christ. But the history of modern and contemporary thought of Judaism is not at issue in this library of Judaism's reading of scripture. Nor is the question of whether or not sages set forth the plain meaning of scripture relevant at all. The concept of a plain, historical, and inherent meaning, as distinct from the fanciful ones invented by the Midrash exegetes, is purely anachronistic. See Raphael Loewe, "The 'Plain' Meaning of scripture in Early Jewish Exegesis," in J. G. Weiss, ed., *Papers of the Institute of Jewish Studies,* London, Volume I (repr. Lanham, Md.: University Press of America/Brown Classics in Judaic Series, 1989), 140–85. The conception of a "'plain' meaning" profoundly misunderstands and misinterprets rabbinic literature.

Preface

Writing with scripture, sages made use of scripture by making it their own and making themselves into the possession of scripture as well, a reciprocal process in which both were changed, each into the likeness and image of the other. This they did by effecting their own selections, shaping a distinctive idiom of discourse, all the while citing, responding to, reflecting upon, scripture's own words in its own context and for its own purpose — the here and now of eternal truth. And through the book of Lamentations our authorship not only wrote with scripture, but set forth a statement that was meant to be coherent and proportioned, well crafted and well composed. Since that statement concerned the distinctively theological question of the validity of the covenant of God with Israel in light of calamities through time, we must classify the writing as theological and find out how, in the compilation before us, the structure accomplished the authorship's goals. This volume of the Bible of Judaism Library aims at doing just that.

I translate the standard printed text. I follow the standard printed text and make constant reference to the first translation of the document, which is A. Cohen, *Lamentations*, in H. Freedman and Maurice Simon, eds., *Midrash Rabbah,* vol. 8 (London: Soncino Press, 1939). In addition I occasionally consulted the text of Salomon Buber, *Midrasch Echa Rabbati. Sammlung agadischer Auslegungen der Klagelieder. Herausgegeben nach einer Handschrift aus der Bibliothek zu Rom cod. J. I. 4, und einer Handschrift des British Museum cod. 27089. Kritisch bearbeitet, kommentiert, und mit einer Einleitung versehen* (Vilna, 1899; repr. Hildesheim: Georg Olms Verlagbuchhandlung, 1967).[1] I know of no better edition even now.[2]

Mine is the second translation of the document, and I systematically consulted the excellent one by A. Cohen. Clearly, I admired Cohen's translation.[3] In the body of my translation, when I use Cohen's translation verbatim, I signify it in this way: [Cohen, p. 00:]. What follows is then his translation, word for word or nearly so, until the opening of a new unit of thought. Cohen's translation seems to me beyond serious complaint for the content of the compilation. In addition, Cohen translated not only Buber's text, but Buber's text in accord with Buber's notes, omitting those passages from his translation that Buber indicates do not occur in the earliest evidences. Where Cohen omits a sizable part of Buber's text, or where Cohen arranges matters in an order different from Buber's, or where he presents a somewhat different wording, I follow Cohen, not Buber. Where I give Cohen's version and not Buber's, I have called attention to that fact. Cohen gives us access to the contents of the compilation, and we owe him much.

But, as I explain in more general terms in my *Translating the Classics of Judaism in Theory and in Practice,* Brown Judaic Studies (Atlanta: Scholars Press, 1989), Cohen's translation is primarily useful as a reference regarding the contents of the document. It makes possible no study of the indicative traits of the document, no definition of the compilation, no analysis of the patterns of rhetoric and logic that characterize this particular piece of writing. Mine makes possible all of these analytical studies. By isolating the smallest whole units of thought, then showing how they comprise propositional discourse, and by highlighting the formal traits of the original through fixed formulas in English, my translation allows for critical inquiry that a translation lacking a reference system does not.

While I present the second translation of Lamentations Rabbah
into English, this is as a matter of fact the first *analytical* translation. By that I mean a simple thing. Unlike Cohen and all prior
translators of rabbinic documents of late antiquity, I offer the text
not as a sequence of undifferentiated columns of words. Rather,
I represent the Hebrew as a set of distinct and discrete compositions put together in one way, one bearing formal and rhetorical
traits.

While taking full advantage of Cohen's reading of the document,
I have found it necessary to retranslate the entire composition. My
intent here is to offer a clear account of the basic statement of the
authorship of Lamentations Rabbah, together with an identification of the components of their writing classified from the smallest
whole units of discourse on upward to completed and coherent
statements. That program accounts for my analytical system, which
marks each smallest whole unit of thought with a letter, completed
propositions of thought (which we might call "paragraphs") with
an Arabic numeral, and entire cogent statements or arguments with
a Roman numeral. In addition to contributing the first usable analytical marking system for every sentence, I also supply a numbering
system in sequence from the beginning to the end of the document
for every completed unit of thought (*petihta* and *parashah* as well),
simply by enumerating every chapter in sequence, beginning to end.
Now people do not have to find a passage identified only as "see
Petihta 23" — which runs on for pages!

The foundation of my analytical translation is the reference system. My reference system allows identification of each complete unit
of thought or other irreducible minimum of discourse, for example, a verse of scripture. On that basis we may clearly perceive the
formal traits of each composite or composition. Until now, to re-
fer to our document we had to use a rather complex system, which
distinguished *petihtaot* (prologues) from *parashiyyot* (chapters), and,
within *parashiyyot*, relied on paragraph and sentence and then a number. Thus, for the Soncino translators in general, I.I.16 stood for
the sixteenth among all of the comments in Lamentations Rabbah
on Lam. 1:1. This seemed to me not felicitous, since a text should
number in one and the same way all of its components. Hence I

have divided the whole into chapters, whether a short *petihta* or a very long *parashah*. I further divided the *parashiyyot* into chapters by reference to the verse that is treated. For example, Lamentations Rabbah to Lam. 1:1 forms a single chapter; then Lamentations Rabbah to Lam. 1:2 likewise. I formed the whole into a single undifferentiated system, as the table of contents makes clear.

I signify with a small (lower-case) Roman numeral the principal components of a given chapter, of which there may be only one or two. That signification is indicated by an Arabic numeral. Thus **XXXV:i.1** alludes to the first major division of the thirty-fifth chapter of the book (which happens to be Lamentations Rabbah to Lam. 1:1). The Arabic numeral then identifies what I conceive to be a complete argument, proposition, syllogism, or fully worked out exegetical exercise (a whole thought). Finally, I point to what I maintain is the smallest whole unit of thought — for example, a sentence or a major component of a sentence, a verse of scripture, a constituent clause of a complex thought, and the like. This is indicated by a letter. Hence **I:i.1.A** alludes to the opening whole unit of thought, in the case at hand, the citation of the base verse, deriving from what happens to be Petihta One.

It remains to acknowledge the sources of biblical verses. I consulted the translations of either *The Oxford Annotated Bible with the Apocrypha: Revised Standard Version*, ed. Herbert G. May and Bruce M. Metzger (New York: Oxford University Press, 1965), or *Tanakh: A New Translation of the Holy Scriptures according to the Traditional Hebrew Text* (Philadelphia: Jewish Publication Society of America, 1985). Many of the translations are my own. Still more are Cohen's, where he has rendered a verse in a way that immediately makes clear the intent of the exegete. So the translations of biblical verses are eclectic.

As to the dating of Lamentations Rabbah, Moses D. Herr ("Midrash," *Encyclopaedia Judaica* 11:1511) places Lamentations Rabbah in the fifth century along with Genesis Rabbah, Leviticus Rabbah, and Esther Rabbah I; he lists as sixth-century compilations Pesiqta deRab Kahana, Songs Rabbah, and Ruth Rabbah.[4]

My debt to my dear friend and co-worker, Dr. Harold Rast, publisher and editor of Trinity Press International, accumulates

now for decades. It suffices to state very simply that he gives academic religious publishing the good name that it deserves; he and
his colleagues at the other principal academic religious presses in
this country have contributed to the shaping of religious dialogue
among informed and literate believers such as, to my knowledge,
has no counterpart in any other country in the world.

I express my thanks also to my friends and colleagues at the University of South Florida. The Department of Religious Studies has
provided for me ideal circumstances in which to teach and study,
and I have found life here more productive than I had imagined life
could be. In times of exceptional financial rigor, the administration
of the University of South Florida has found it possible to support
my research through provision of special funds and also through
the remarkably generous terms of my appointment as Distinguished
Research Professor of Religious Studies. It remains my task to be
worthy of my opportunities; I do not think that, in times past or
even today, many scholars have enjoyed so favorable a situation as
USF has made for me.

Since I discuss my work from day to day with Professor William
Scott Green, University of Rochester, since the idea of "writing
with scripture" was born in conversations with him, and since the
phrase itself is his, I am happy to point also to his fundamental con-
tributions to this work and to the library of which it forms the third
volume.

Jacob Neusner

Notes

1. Moses D. Herr ("Lamentations Rabbah," *Encyclopaedia Judaica* 10:
1378) comments, "Buber published a scholarly edition, based on manuscripts, with an introduction and notes. Despite its defects and inaccuracies
it represented at the time a considerable advance. Most of the manuscripts
of the Midrash have not thus far been utilized."

2. Avigdor Shinan, Hebrew University of Jerusalem, confirms that there
is at this time no critical text. But I wanted my translation to relate first
of all to Cohen's, which I found exceedingly helpful, and in addition I
wanted my translation to work well for those who have in hand the familiar

standard Hebrew text and not Buber's. There is a measure of eclecticism, in that occasionally I adopted Buber's formulations of a passage, while in the main presenting the standard Hebrew printed text in faithful accord with Cohen's reading of it. That occasionally eclectic approach, moreover, may produce a bit of confusion. But it is not the task of translators to create and only then translate a critical text. A translation serves best, so I conceive, when the text that is translated is in the hands of those likely to consult both the translation and the original Hebrew. The upshot for this document is simple. Until we have a critical text, such as is presently under way, I am told, in the Hebrew University of Jerusalem, any translation must serve only provisionally and then carry out the quite clearly defined purposes of the translator.

3. I take note also of S. Dunsky, *Midrash Rabbah. Echah. (Lamentations), with Yiddish Translation, Explanatory Notes, and Introduction* (Montreal: Northern Printing and Lithographing Co., 1956). I did not make use of this work.

4. But the entire conception of what we mean by a "date" for a document in the canon of the Judaism of the dual Torah, and how we date a Midrash compilation in particular, requires explanation. It suffices for the present purpose simply to repeat the conventional facts, such as Herr provides. Specifically, Herr describes the whole group as follows: "These Midrashim all consist of a collection of homilies, sayings, and aggadot of the amoraim (and also of the tannaim) in Galilean Aramaic and rabbinical Hebrew, but they also include many Greek words. It seems that all these Midrashim, which are not mentioned in the Babylonian Talmud, were edited in Erez Israel in the fifth and sixth centuries C.E. Two types can be distinguished: exegetical and homiletical. The exegetical Midrash (Genesis Rabbah, Lamentations Rabbah, et al.) is a Midrash to one of the books of the Bible, containing comments on the whole book — on each chapter, on every verse, and at times on every word in the verse. The homiletical Midrash is either a Midrash to a book of the Pentateuch in which only the first verse . . . of the weekly portion is expounded . . . (e.g., Leviticus Rabbah), or a Midrash that is based only on the biblical and prophetic reading of special Sabbaths . . . in which, also, only the first verses are expounded (e.g., Pirkei deRav Kahana). In both cases in contrast to the exegetical Midrashim, the homiletical Midrashim contain almost no short homilies or dicta on variegated topics, but each chapter . . . constitutes a collection of homilies and sayings on one topic that seem to combine into one long homily on the specific topic" ("Midrash," p. 1510). Herr states ("Lamentations Rabbah," *Encyclopaedia Judaica* 10:1376–78), "Except for some later additions, the entire Midrash, including the poems, is a compilation redacted by a single redactor. No sage later than the fourth century is mentioned in it. . . . The

redactor used tannaitic literature, the Jerusalem Talmud, Genesis Rabbah
and Leviticus Rabbah. Lamentations Rabbah itself was used as a source
for Ruth Rabbah and probably also for Pesikta deRav Kahana, as well as
for later Midrashim. In view of this and of its language, it was appar-
ently redacted in Erez Israel at about the end of the fifth century C.E." I
am not sure what Herr means when he claims that this is "a compilation
redacted by a single redactor," but that is a matter to be dealt with in its
own context.

1

Israel in Time and Eternity
The Message of
Lamentations Rabbah

The Judaic sages saw the everyday as a recapitulation of scripture in the here and the now. Witnessing an event in the street, they perceived a rehearsal of an event in scripture. Or they understood the event and its meaning in the model of what they deemed to be scripture's counterpart and parable. So they formed a single eternity out of disparate time — theirs present and the past of history. Through scriptural study they accomplished that recasting of the here and the now into the model of eternity. So they approached scripture to help them see the everyday as a recapitulation of scripture, but also, and I think of equal consequence, scripture as the matrix for the everyday. They took the position that we understand scripture better than did a generation before us, as they understood matters better than did their predecessors; for each succeeding age knows more than the one before about God's plan for all time and all humanity. If I may express what I conceive to be their conception of matters: We are not wiser because we know more, but in the pages of scripture we

1

may become wiser by understanding better what we know. All of this is meant to be captured by the phrase "writing with scripture."

When we contemplate the result of writing with scripture — here, the messages our authorship presented in the setting of an encounter with the book of Lamentations — we see work of considerable originality and striking cogency. But we should err if we maintained that our authorship, among many, merely said in their own words and in the words of scripture what scripture said anyhow. Nothing could be further from the point. Once a process of selection commences and a labor of system construction begins, then the materials at hand are relegated to merely that: the raw materials of building what is the work, in the end, of the architects, engineers, and laborers. As soon as an authorship does more than repeat what it finds in scripture — and that authorship that merely apes or copies is no authorship at all — we enter the realm of those who write with scripture.

Sages in the canonical writings of the Judaism of the dual Torah appealed to scripture not merely for proof texts as part of an apologia, but for a far more original and sustained mode of discourse. In constant interchange with scripture, they found ways of delivering their own message, in their own idiom, and in diverse ways. Verses of scripture therefore served not merely to prove but to instruct. Israelite scripture constituted not merely a source of validation but a powerful instrument of profound inquiry. And the propositions that could be proposed, the statements that could be made, prove diverse. Scripture served as a kind of syntax, limiting the arrangement of words but making possible an infinity of statements. The upshot is that the received scriptures formed an instrumentality for the expression of an authorship responsible for a writing bearing its own integrity and cogency, an authorship appealing to its own conventions of intelligibility, and, above all, making its own points. Our authorship did not write *about* scripture, creating, for example, a literature of commentary and exegesis essentially within the program of scripture. Rather, they wrote *with* scripture. And that they did in many ways.

Let us now survey the messages that they presented in this dialogue with scripture. In the abstract I see three principal topics on which our authorship presents its propositions, of which the first three correspond to the three relationships into which the sages' world, that is, Israel, entered: with heaven, with earth, and with its own existence. These yield, for our rubrics, systematic statements that concern the relationships between (1) Israel and God, with special reference to the covenant, the Torah, and the land; (2) Israel and the nations, with interest in Israel's history, past, present, and future, and how that cycle is to be known; and (3) Israel on its own terms, with focus upon Israel's distinctive leadership.

Israel and God

The principal theme of our compilation is Israel's relationship with God, and the principal message concerning that theme is that the stipulative covenant still and always governs that relationship. Therefore everything that happens to Israel makes sense and bears meaning; and Israel is not helpless before its fate but controls its own destiny. This is the whole message of our compilation, and it is the only message that is repeated throughout; everything else proves secondary and derivative of the fundamental proposition that the destruction proves the enduring validity of the covenant, its rules, and its promise of redemption. Let us now move, beginning to end, through the many passages that upon inspection prove to say that one thing. We work sequentially, in accord with the order of the verses of the document *petihtaot* [prologues] through the end of chapter 4; in any event I see no logical sequence dictated by the inner structure of the single theme and proposition at hand.

Israel's relationship with God is treated with special reference to the covenant, the Torah, and the land. By reason of the sins of the Israelites, they have gone into exile with the destruction of the Temple. The founders of the family, Abraham, Isaac, and Jacob, also went into exile. Now they cannot be accused of lacking in religious duties, attention to teachings of the Torah and of prophecy, carrying out the requirements of righteousness (philanthropy) and good deeds, and the like. The people are at fault for their own condition (I:i.1–7). Torah study defines the condition of Israel, e.g., "If you have seen [the inhabitants of] towns uprooted from their places in the land of Israel, know that it is because they did not pay the salary of scribes and teachers" (II.i).

So long as Judah and Benjamin were at home, God could take comfort at the loss of the ten tribes; once they went into exile, God began to mourn (II:ii). Israel survived Pharaoh and Sennacherib, but not God's punishment (III:i). After the disaster in Jeremiah's time, Israel emerged from Eden — but could come back (IV:i). God did not play favorites among the tribes; when any of them sinned, he punished them through exile (VI:i). Israel was punished because of the ravaging of words of Torah and prophecy, righteous men, religious duties, and good deeds (VII:i). The land of Israel, the Torah, and the Temple are ravaged, to the shame of Israel (Jer. 9:19–21) (VIII:i). The Israelites practiced idolatry more than did the pagans; God was neglected by the people and was left solitary, so God responded to the people's actions (X:i). If you had achieved the merit (using the theological language at hand), then you would have enjoyed everything, but since you did not have the merit, you enjoyed nothing (XI:i).

The Israelites did not trust God, so they suffered disaster (XIII.i). The Israelites scorned God and brought dishonor upon God among the nations (XV:i). While God was generous with the Israelites in the wilderness, under severe conditions, he was harsh with them in civilization, under pleasant conditions, because they sinned and angered him (XVI:i). With merit one drinks good water in Jerusalem; without, bad water in the exile of Babylonia. With merit one sings songs and psalms in Jerusalem; without, dirges and lamentations in Babylonia. At stake is peoples' merit, not God's grace (XIX:i). The contrast is drawn between redemption and disaster, the giving of the Torah and the destruction of the Temple (XX:i). When the Israelites went into exile among the nations of the world, not one of them could produce a word of Torah from his mouth; God punished Israel for its sins (XXI:i). Idolatry was the cause (XXII:i). The destruction of the Temple was possible only because God had already abandoned it (XXIV:ii). When the Temple was destroyed, God was answerable to the patriarchs for what he had done (XXIV:ii). The Presence of God departed from the Temple by stages (XXV:i).

The Holy One punishes Israel only after bringing testimony

against them (XXVII:i). The road that led from the salvation of
Hezekiah is the one that brought Israel to the disaster brought about
by Nebuchadnezzar. Then the Israelite kings believed, but the pagan
king did not believe; and God gave the Israelite kings a reward for
their faith, through Hezekiah, and to the pagan king, who did not
believe or obey, were handed over Jerusalem and its Temple (XXX:i).
Before the Israelites went into exile, the Holy One, blessed be he,
called them bad. But when they had gone into exile, he began to
sing their praises (XXXI:i). The Israelites were sent into exile only
after they had sinned against the Unique One of the world, the Ten
Commandments, circumcision, which had been given to the twentieth generation [Abraham], and the Pentateuch (XXXV:ii, iii). When
the Temple was destroyed and Israel went into exile, God mourned
in the manner that mortals do (XXXV:iv). The prophetic critique of
Israel is mitigated by mercy. There is no proof that just as the Israelites did not go to extremes in sinning, so the measure of justice
did not do so. Israel stands in an ambiguous relationship with God,
both divorced and not divorced (XXXV:vi, vii).

Before God penalizes, he has already prepared the healing for
the penalty. As to all the harsh prophecies that Jeremiah issued
against the Israelites, Isaiah first of all anticipated each and pronounced healing for it (XXXVI:ii). The Israelites err for weeping
frivolously, "but in the end there will be a real weeping for good
cause" (XXXVI:iv, v). The ten tribes went into exile, but the Presence of God did not go into exile. Judah and Benjamin went into
exile, but the Presence of God did not go into exile. But when the
children went into exile, then the Presence of God went into exile (XXXIX:iii). The great men of Israel turned their faces away
when they saw people sinning, and God did the same to them
(XL:ii). When the Israelites carry out the will of the Holy One,
they add strength to the strength of heaven, and when they do
not, they weaken the power of the One above (XL:ii). The exile
and the redemption will match (XL:ii). In her affliction, Jerusalem
remembered her rebellion against God (XLI:i).

When the gentile nations sin, there is no sequel in punishment,
but when the Israelites sin, they also are punished (XLII:i). God
considered carefully how to bring the evil upon Israel (XLVIII:i).

God suffers with Israel and for Israel (L:i), a minor theme in a massive compilation of stories. By observing their religious duties the Israelites became distinguished before God (LIII:i). With every thing with which the Israelites sinned, they were smitten, and with that same thing they will be comforted. When they sinned with the head, they were smitten at the head, but they were comforted through the head (LVI:i). There is an exact match between Israel's triumph and Israel's downfall. Thus, just as these were punished through the destruction effected by priest and prophet (the priests and Joshua at Jericho), so these were subject to priest and prophet (Jeremiah). Just as these were punished through the ram's horn and shouting, so Israel will be through ram's horn and shouting (LVII:ii).

God's relationship to Israel was complicated by the relationship to Jacob: "Isn't it the fact that the Israelites are angering me only because of the icon of Jacob that is engraved on my throne? Here, take it, it's thrown in your face!" (LVII:ii). God is engaged with Israel's disaster (LIX:ii). The Israelites did not fully explore the limits of the measure of justice, so the measure of justice did not go to extremes against them (LX:i, LXI:i). God's decree against Jerusalem comes from of old (LXIV:i). God forewarned Israel and showed Israel favor, but it did no good (LXIX:i). God did to Israel precisely what he had threatened long ago (LXXIII:i). But God does not rejoice in punishing Israel (LXXIII:i). The argument between God and Israel is framed in this way: the Community of Israel says that they are the only ones who accepted God; God says, I rejected everybody else for you (LXXIX:ii). Israel accepted its suffering as atonement and asked that the suffering expiate the sin (LXXV:i).

God suffers along with Israel, Israel's loyalty will be recognized and appreciated by God, and, in the meantime, the Israelites will find in the Torah the comfort that they require. The nations will be repaid for their actions toward Israel in the interval. Even though the Holy One, blessed be he, is angry with his servants, the righteous, in this world, in the world to come he has mercy on them (LXXXVI:i). God is good to those that deserve it (LXXXVII:i). God mourns for Israel the way human mourners mourn (LXXXVIII:i). God will never abandon Israel (LXXXIX:i).

The Holy Spirit brings about redemption (XCV:i). It is better to be punished by God than favored by a gentile king: "Better was the removing of the ring by Pharaoh [for the sealing of decrees to oppress the Israelites] than the forty years during which Moses prophesied concerning them, because it was through this [oppression] that the redemption came about, while through that [prophesying] the redemption did not come about" (CXXII:i).

The upshot here is that persecution in the end is good for Israel, because it produces repentance more rapidly than prophecy ever did, with the result that the redemption is that much nearer. The enemy will also be punished for its sins, and, further, God's punishment is appropriate and well-placed. People get what they deserve, both Israel and the others. God should protect Israel and not leave them among the nations, but that is not what he has done (CXXIII:i). God blames that generation for its own fate, and the ancestors claim that the only reason the Israelites endure is because of the merit of the ancestors (CXXIX:i). The redemption of the past tells us about the redemption in the future (CXXX:i). "The earlier generations, because they smelled the stench of only part of the tribulations inflicted by the idolatrous kingdoms, became impatient. But we, who dwell in the midst of the four kingdoms, how much the more so [are we impatient]!" (CXXXI:i).

God's redemption is certain, so people who are suffering should be glad, since that is a guarantee of coming redemption: "For if those who outrage him he treats in such a way, those who do his will all the more so!" So if the words of Uriah are carried out, the words of Zechariah will be carried out, while if the words of Uriah prove false, then the words of Zechariah will not be true either. "I was laughing with pleasure because the words of Uriah have been carried out, and that means that the words of Zechariah in the future will be carried out" (CXL:i). The Temple will be restored, and Israel will regain its place, as God's throne and consort, respectively (CXLI:i). Punishment and rejection will be followed by forgiveness and reconciliation (CXLII:i). The Jews can accomplish part of the task on their own, even though they throw themselves wholly on God's mercy. The desired age is either like that of Adam, or like that of Moses and Solomon, or like that of Noah and Abel. All three possibilities link the coming redemption to a time of perfection, Eden; or to the age prior to idolatry; or to the time of Moses and Solomon, the builders of the cult and the Temple, respectively (CXLIII:i).

The end says it all: if there is rejection, there is no hope, but if there is anger, there is hope, because someone who is angry may in the end be appeased. Whenever there is an allusion to divine anger, that too is a mark of hope (CXLIV:i).

Israel and the Nations

Israel's relationship with the nations is treated with interest in Israel's history, past, present, and future, and in how that cycle is to be known. But there is no theory of "the other" or the outsider here: the nations are the enemy; the compilers find nothing of merit to report about them. Israel's difference from the other, for which God is responsible, accounts for the dislike that the nations express toward Israel; Israel's present condition as minority, different and despised on account of the difference, is God's fault and choice. Israel was besieged not only by the Babylonians but also by its neighbors, the Ammonites and Moabites (IX:i), and God will punish them too. The public ridicule of the Jews' religious rites contrasts with the Jews' own perception of their condition. The exposition of Psalm 69:13 in terms of the gentiles' ridicule of the Jews' practices — the Jews' poverty, their Sabbath and Seventh Year observance — is followed by a re-exposition of the Jews' practices, now with respect to the ninth of Ab (XVII:i). Even though the nations of the world go into exile, their exile is not really an exile at all. But as for Israel, their exile really is an exile. The nations of the world, who eat the bread and drink the wine of others, do not really experience exile. But the Israelites, who do not eat the bread and drink the wine of others, really do experience exile (XXXVII:i).

The Ammonites and Moabites joined with the enemy and behaved very spitefully (XLIV:i). When the Israelites fled from the destruction of Jerusalem, the nations of the world sent word to every place to which they fled and shut them out (LV:i). But this was to be blamed on God: "If we had intermarried with them, they would have accepted us" (LXIX:i). There are ten references to the "might" of Israel; when the Israelites sinned, these forms of might were taken away from them and given to the nations of the world. The nations of the world ridicule the Jews for their religious observances (LXXXIII:i).

These propositions simply expose, in their own framework, the same propositions as those concerning God's relationship to Israel and Israel's relationship to God. The relationship between Israel and the nations forms a subset of the relationship of Israel and God; nothing in the former relationship happens on its own, but all things express in this mundane context the rules and effects of the rules that govern in the transcendent relationship. All we learn about Israel and the nations is that the covenant endures, bearing its own inevitable sanctions and consequences.

Israel on Its Own

Our authorship has little interest in Israel outside of relationship with either God or the nations. Israel on its own forms a subordinated and trivial theme; whatever messages we do find take on meaning only in the initial framework, that defined by Israel's relationship with God. Israel is never on its own.

The bitterness of the ninth of Ab is contrasted with the bitter herbs with which the first redemption is celebrated (XVIII:i). The same contrast is drawn between the giving of the Torah and the destruction of the Temple (XX:i). If Israel had found rest among the nations, it would not have returned to the holy land (XXXVII:ii). The glory of Israel lay in its relationship to God, in the sanhedrin, in the disciples of sages, in the priestly watches, in the children (XL:i). Israel first suffers, then rejoices; its unfortunate condition marks the fact that Israel stands at the center of things (LIX:iii). Israel has declined through the generations: "In olden times, when people held the sanhedrin in awe, naughty words were never included in songs. But when the sanhedrin was abolished, naughty words were inserted in songs. In olden times, when troubles came upon Israel, they stopped rejoicing on that account. Now that both have come to an end [no more singing, no more banquet halls], 'The joy of

our hearts has ceased; our dancing has been turned to mourning'"
(CXXXVII:i).

Now to the encounter with a remarkable document, which trans-
forms the calamity of an hour into a lesson for eternity — changing
history not into what we now call social science, but what, had they
used our language and categories, our sages would have called theology. The immediate relevance of the book of Lamentations to
twenty-first century people hardly requires much explanation. The
world still mourns the destruction of European Jewry in World
War II, when approximately six million Jews were systematically
murdered by the Germans as a critical component of their war
against humanity. When we read the book of Lamentations, it
speaks of fresh sorrows and unhealed wounds; every line in that
mournful book sustains a commentary on the tragedy of our own
times. And as we follow Lamentations Rabbah, we see how our
sages of blessed memory read the book of Lamentations just as we
do, and with as much reason: it was an account of what happened
to them, of how their world was changed.

2

Petihta One

Alas! Lonely sits the city once great with people!

We begin with the most striking approach to the reading of scripture that our sages explore: the "intersecting verse / base verse" form. In this form, we ignore the verse under discussion, dealing with a different verse from a different book altogether. We work on the theme of that verse, systematically interpreting it and underlining its implications. Only then, at the end, do we approach what I call the "base verse," namely, the verse of the book under study (in our case, Lamentations), and then we read that base verse in light of the perspective set forth in the intersecting one. In the present instance, Abba bar Kahana reads Lamentations 1:1 in light of Isaiah 10:30. What we shall see is how that "intersecting verse" imposes upon the "base verse" a completely fresh point, so that what we thought the verse meant to say turns out to conceal a much deeper layer of meaning. To understand the intersecting verse / base verse mode of exegesis, we must recall that our exegetes dismantle the whole of scripture into its parts: the books into their verses, the verses into their phrases, and on downward. In reading one verse of scripture, we have every right — so the theory of the single, coherent revelation or Torah will allow — to turn to any other verse of scripture to clarify the original, or base, verse.

I.i.
1. A. R. Abba bar Kahana opened [by citing the following verse of scripture], "'Cry with a shrill voice, O daughter of Gallim [hearken, Laishah! Take up the cry, Anathoth!]' (Is. 10:30).
   B. "Said Isaiah [printed text: Jeremiah] to Israel, 'Instead of saying songs and psalms before an idol, "Cry with a shrill voice, O daughter of Gallim" (Is. 10:30).
   C. "'Cry with a shrill voice' in synagogues."

The implicit theodicy, defending the destruction of the Temple in the time of Jeremiah, is straightforward: Israel cried out before idols but should cry out in the synagogue instead. We will now work out the meaning of the phrases of the intersecting verse, finding a variety of meanings ("another matter" or "another teaching"). But these, we rapidly observe, turn out to go over the same point time and again, so what is that "other matter" is another way of demonstrating the same point.

2. A. ["Cry with a shrill voice, O daughter of Gallim" (Is. 10:30):]
   B. "Daughter of Gallim" [the Hebrew word *gallim* may be rendered "waves"]:
   C. just as waves are readily discerned in the sea, so your forebears are readily discerned in the world.
3. A. ["Cry with a shrill voice, O daughter of Gallim" (Is. 10:30):]
   B. Another teaching concerning "[Daughter of] Gallim":
   C. daughter of those who go into exile [reading instead of Gallim, *Golim*, the exiles].
   D. [Aramaic:] daughter of exiles, daughter of Abraham, concerning whom it is written, "And there was a famine in the land; and Abram went down into Egypt" (Gen. 12:10).

    E. Daughter of Isaac: "And Isaac went to Abimelech, king of the Philistines, to Gerar" (Gen. 26:1).

    F. Daughter of Jacob: "And he went to Paddan-aram" (Gen. 28:5).

4. A. "...hearken, [Laishah]":

    B. "Hearken to the religious duties."

    C. "Hearken to teachings of the Torah."

    D. "Hearken to teachings of prophecy."

    E. "Hearken to the requirements of righteousness and good deeds."

5. A. "[...hearken, Laishah:]"

    B. And if not, there will be a *laishah*, that is, a lion will attack you.

    C. This refers to Nebuchadnezzar, the wicked man, concerning whom it is written, "A lion is gone up from his thicket" (Jer. 4:7).

6. A. "...Take up the cry, [Anathoth!]" (Is. 10:30):

    B. [Reading the word for "take up the cry" with the same consonants but different vowels, the meaning becomes "impoverished," thus:] impoverished in righteous person,

    C. impoverished in teachings of the Torah,

    D. impoverished in teachings of prophecy,

    E. impoverished in religious duties and good deeds.

7. A. "[Take up the cry,] Anathoth!" (Is. 10:30):

    B. And if not, Anathoth, that is, the man of Anatoth, will come and prophesy against you words of rebuke,

    C. as it is written, "The words of Jeremiah, son of Hiliah of the priests who were in Anathoth" (Jer. 1:1).

    D. Since retribution has come, [Jeremiah] laments for them: "Alas! Lonely sits the city once great with people!" (Lam. 1:1).

The contribution of the form is twofold. First, the exegete wishes to lead us to the base verse, which is the same for all of the proems, "Alas! Lonely sits the city once great with people!" (Lam. 1:1). Second, he wishes to lead us to that verse through an exposition of Isaiah 10:30, a verse chosen for obvious reasons. Then the point he

proposes to make is that by reason of the sins of the Israelites, they
have gone into exile with the destruction of the Temple. But this
point is made in a somewhat odd way, since we begin, with No. 3,
not with a repertoire of sins, but rather with the affirmation that
the founders of the family, Abraham, Isaac, and Jacob, also went
into exile. Now they cannot be accused of lacking in religious duties, attention to teachings of the Torah and prophecy, carrying out
the requirements of righteousness (philanthropy) and good deeds,
and the like. But the point of Nos. 4, 5, 6 is precisely that. The upshot is that there are two distinct themes in play: one, the descent
from the patriarchs (the matriarchs rarely occur), the other, the fault
of the people for their own condition, the whole then leading us to
Jeremiah, author of Lamentations. The complexity is not in proposition but in exposition, and the art makes readily accessible the main
point while making that point in a subtle way through the interplay
of the verses Isaiah 10:30 and Jeremiah 1:1. Then, in 7.D, comes
the fixed conclusion, which is necessary to complete the whole. The
message is a rich and engaging one, leaving no doubt through the
myriad of details of its one simple point.

3

Petihta Twenty-Three

So appreciate your Creator in the days of your youth,
before those days of sorrow come and those years arrive
of which you will say, "I have no pleasure in them."

The *petihta,* or prologue, addresses not our base verse alone, but the theme of the book of Lamentations in general. So we have to supply a base verse at the end of a long and systematic interpretation of the intersecting verse. In the present instance, our attention is drawn to Qohelet [=Ecclesiastes] 12:1–8. Solomon speaks, conveying a mood of remorse. In our reading of the passage, the message of sorrow carries over from the aged king to the defeated people.

XXIII.i.

1. A. R. Joshua of Siknin in the name of R. Levi commenced [by citing the following verse of scripture]: "'So appreciate your Creator in the days of your youth' ["So appreciate your Creator in the days of your youth, before those days of sorrow come and those years arrive of which you will say, 'I have no pleasure in them,' before sun

15

and light and moon and stars grow dark, and the clouds come back again after the rain: When the guards of the house become shaky, and the men of valor are bent, and the maids that grind grow few, are idle, and the ladies that peer through the windows grow dim, and the doors to the street are shut — with the noise of the hand mill growing fainter, and the song of the bird growing feebler, and all the strains of music dying down; when one is afraid of heights, and there is terror on the road — for the almond tree may blossom, the grasshopper be burden, and the caper bush may bud again; but man sets out for his eternal abode with mourners all around in the street — Before the silver cord snaps, and the golden bowl crashes, the jar is shattered at the spring, and the jug is smashed at the cistern, and the dust returns to the ground as it was, and the lifebreath returns to God who bestowed it. Utterly futility, said Koheleth, all is futile!" (Qohelet 12:1–8):]

B. "Said Solomon to Israel, ' "Appreciate your Creator": Remember your creation while your selection endures [the words for "youth" and "selection" share the same consonants].

C. " 'while the covenant of the priesthood endures: "And I chose him out of all the tribes of Israel to be my priest" (1 Sam. 2:28);

D. " 'while the covenant of the Levites still endures: "The city which I have chosen" (1 Kgs. 11:32);

E. " 'while the covenant with the kingdom of the house of David endures: "He chose David as his servant" (Ps. 78:70);

F. " 'while the covenant with Jerusalem endures: "The city which I have chosen" (1 Kgs. 11:32);

G. " 'while the covenant with the house of the sanctuary endures: "For now I have chosen and sanctified this house" (2 Chr. 7:16);

H. " 'while you still endure: "The Lord your God has chosen you" ' (Dt. 7:6)."

2. A. "before those days of sorrow come":

B. this refers to the days of exile.

3. A. "and those years arrive of which you will say, 'I have no pleasure in them'":

B. neither good nor bad.

4. A. "before sun [and light and moon and stars] grow dark":

B. this refers to the kingdom of the house of David: "And his throne as the sun before me" (Ps. 89:37).

5. A. "and light":

B. this refers to the light of the Torah: "For the commandment is a lamp and the Torah is a light" (Prov. 6:23).

6. A. "and moon":

B. this refers to the sanhedrin: The sanhedrin is seated in the shape of a semi-circular threshing floor [M. Sanh. 4:3].

7. A. "and stars":

B. this refers to the rabbis: "They who turn the many to righteousness are as the stars for ever and ever" (Dan. 12:3).

8. A. "and the clouds come back again after the rain":

B. You find that all of the most harsh and terrible prophecies that Jeremiah prophesied concerning them were issued only after the destruction of the Temple.

9. A. "When the guards of the house become shaky":

B. these are the priestly and Levitical watches.

10. A. "and the men of valor are bent":

B. this refers to the priests.

Our document bears in the body of the text materials that, in our time, go into footnotes; since the framers of this writing had no technical means of indicating footnotes, they placed them in the text itself. To show how coherent their document is, once we recognize extraneous materials for what they are, I indent footnote materials. The same is so for occasional appendices, long compilations of materials on a given topic that do not advance the point being made but that our sages did regard as important. These too are indented.

C. [The following statements are meant to illustrate the exceptional strength of the priests:] Said R. Abba b. Kahana, "Twenty-two thousand Levites did Aaron consecrate on a single day: 'And Aaron offered them as a sacred gift before the Lord' (Num. 8:21)."

D. Said R. Hanina, "The bird's crop is very light, but the priest could throw it to the ramp, thirty-two cubits away."

11. A. "and the maids that grind grow few, are idle":

B. this refers to the great Mishnah compilations,

C. for instance, the Mishnah compilation of R. Aqiba,

D. and the Mishnah compilation of R. Hoshaiah,

E. and the Mishnah compilation of Bar Qappara.

12. A. "grow few":

B. This refers to the Talmud, which is contained in them.

13. A. "and the ladies that peer through the windows grow dim":

B. You find that when the Israelites went into exile among the nations of the world, not a single one of them could remember his disciples [better: his learning].

14. A. "and the doors to the street are shut":

B. this refers to the doors of Nehusta, son of Elnathan, which had been opened wide.

15. A. "with the noise of the hand mill growing fainter":

B. This was because they did not occupy themselves with the words of the Torah.

C. Said R. Samuel b. Nahman, "The Israelites are compared to millstones.

D. "Just as millstones are never left idle, so the Israelites are never idle in regard to the Torah, neither by day nor by night: 'You shall meditate therein day and night' (Josh. 1:8)."

16. A. "and the song of the bird growing feebler":

B. this refers to the wicked Nebuchadnezzar.

C. Said Rabbi, "For eighteen years an echo went forth in the palace of Nebuchadnezzar, saying, 'Wicked servant! Go and destroy the house of your master, for his children are not obedient to him.'"

17. A. "and all the strains of music dying down":

B. So [Nebuchadnezzar] went up and ended singing from banquet houses: "They will not drink wine with a song" (Is. 24:9).

18. A. "when one is afraid of heights":

B. [Nebuchadnezzar] was afraid of the Highest One of the world.

C. He said, "He plans only to trap me to do to me what he did to my ancestor."

19. A. "and there is terror on the road":

B. R. Abba bar Kahana and R. Levi:

C. R. Abba bar Kahana said, "The fear of travel affected him."

D. R. Levi said, "He began to consult [following Cohen, p. 31] charmers on the way."

20. A. [Amplifying 19.D:] For the king of Babylon has stood at the fork of the road, [where two roads branch off, to perform divination. He has shaken arrows, consulted teraphim, and inspected the liver. In his right hand came up the omen against Jerusalem, to set battering rams, to proclaim murder, to raise battle shouts, to set battering rams against the gates, to cast up mounds, to erect towers. In their eyes, the oaths they had sworn to them were like empty divination; but this shall serve to recall their guilt, for which they shall be taken to task]" (Ez. 21:25–28):

B. at a parting of the way.

C. "where two roads branch off ":

D. one goes to the wilderness, the other to Jerusalem.

E. "to perform divination":

F. that is what he began to do.

G. "He has shaken arrows":

H. one had the name of Rome, with no result; one had the name of Alexandria, with no result; one had the name of Jerusalem, and that one came up.

I. He sowed seed and planted plants with the name of Rome, with no result; he sowed seed and planted plants with the name of Alexandria, with no result; with the name of Jerusalem, and the plants came up and flourished.

J. He lit candles and lamps in the name of Rome, and they gave no light, in the name of Alexandria, and they gave no light, in the name of Jerusalem, and they gave light.

K. "consulted teraphim":

L. that refers to his idol: "And stubbornness is as idolatry and teraphim" (1 Sam. 15:23).

M. "and inspected the liver":

N. Said R. Levi, "It is like an Arab who killed a lamb and looked at the liver."

O. "In his right hand came up the omen against Jerusalem":

P. the lot for Jerusalem came up in his right hand.

Q. "to set battering rams": generals.

R. "to proclaim murder": executioners.

S. "to raise battle shouts,": trumpets.

T. "to set battering rams against the gates": observation posts.

U. "to cast up mounds": catapults.

V. "to erect towers": scaling ladders.

W. "In their eyes, the oaths they had sworn to them were like empty divination":

X. Said Ezekiel to the Israelites, "Had you attained merit, you would have recited in the Torah, which is interpreted seven times seven ways, but now that you have not attained merit, lo, Nebuchadnezzar is coming to conduct divination against you in seven times seven ways."

Y. That is in line with this verse: "the oaths they had sworn to them" [Cohen: who have weeks upon weeks"].

21. A. "... but this shall serve to recall their guilt, for which they shall be taken to task" (Ez. 21:28):

B. This refers to the sin committed against Zechariah: "Then the spirit of God enveloped Zechariah son of Jehoiada the priest; he stood above the people [and said to them, 'Thus God said: Why do you transgress the commandments of the Lord when you cannot succeed? Since you have forsaken the Lord, he has forsaken you.' They conspired against him and pelted him with stones in the court of the house of the Lord by the order of the king. King Joash disregarded the loyalty that his father Jehoiada had shown to him and killed his son. As he was dying, he said, 'May the Lord see and requite it']" (2 Chr. 24:20–22):

C. Was he above the people? But he saw himself higher than the whole people, as son-in-law of the king, high priest, prophet, and judge.

D. He began to address them in an arrogant way: "Thus God said: 'Why do you transgress the commandments of the Lord when you cannot succeed? Since you have forsaken the Lord, he has forsaken you.' They conspired against him and pelted him with stones in the court of the house of the Lord by the order of the king."

E. But they did not dispose of his blood like the blood of a hin or a ram: "He shall pour out the blood thereof and cover it with dust" (Lev. 17:13).

F. Here: "her blood is in the midst of her" (Ez. 24:7).

G. Why so? "but this shall serve to recall their guilt, for which they shall be taken to task."

22. A. R. Yudan asked R. Aha, "Where did the Israelites kill Zechariah? Was it in the courtyard of women or in the courtyard of the Israelites?"

B. He said to him, "It was neither in the women's courtyard nor in the Israelites' courtyard, but in the priests' courtyard.

C. "But they did not dispose of his blood like the blood of a hin or a ram: 'He shall pour out the blood thereof and cover it with dust' (Lev. 17:13).

D. "But here: 'For the blood she shed is still in her; she set it upon a bare rock; she did not pour it out on the ground to cover it with earth' (Ez. 24:7).

E. "'She set her blood upon the bare rock, so that it was not covered, so that it may stir up my fury to take vengeance' (Ez. 24:8)."

23. A. Seven transgressions did the Israelites commit on that day: they murdered [1] a priest, [2] prophet, [3] judge, [4] they spilled innocent blood, [5] they blasphemed the divine name, [6] they imparted uncleanness to the courtyard, and it was, furthermore, [7] a Day of Atonement that coincided with the Sabbath.

B. When Nebuzaradan came in, the blood began to drip. He said to them, "What sort of blood is this dripping blood?"

C. They said to him, "It is the blood of oxen, rams, and sheep that we offered on the altar."

D. He forthwith sent and brought oxen, rams, and sheep and slaughtered them in his presence, but the blood continued to drip.

E. He said to them, "If you tell the truth, well and good, but if not, I shall comb your flesh with iron combs."

F. They said to him, "What shall we tell you? He was a prophet who rebuked us. We conspired against him and killed him. And lo, years have passed, but his blood has not stopped seething."

G. He said to them, "I shall appease it."

H. He brought before him the great sanhedrin and the lesser sanhedrin and killed them, until their blood mingled with that of Zechariah: "Oaths are imposed and broken, they kill and rob, there is nothing but adultery and licence, one deed of blood after another" (Hos. 4:2).

I. Still the blood seethed. He brought boys and girls and killed them by the blood, but it did not stop seething.

J. He brought youngsters from the school house and killed them over it, but it did not stop seething.

K. Forthwith he took eighty thousand young priests and killed them on his account, until the blood lapped the grave of Zechariah. But the blood did not stop seething.

L. He said, "Zechariah, Zechariah, All the best of them I have destroyed. Do you want me to exterminate them all?"

M. When he said this, the blood forthwith came to rest.

N. Then he considered repenting, saying, "Now if one soul matters so, as to that man who has killed all these souls, how much the more so!"

O. He fled and sent a parting gift and converted.

24. A. "for the almond tree may blossom":

B. this refers to the prophecy of Jeremiah: "The word of the Lord came to me: What do you see, Jeremiah? I said, I see a branch of an almond tree. The Lord said to me, You have seen right. For I am watchful to bring my word to pass" (Jer. 1:11–12).

C. Said R. Eleazar, "What is the symbol of the almond tree?

D. "From the time that it begins to blossom until it finishes are twenty-one days.

E. "So too from the seventeenth of Tammuz until the ninth of Ab are twenty-one days."

25. A. "the grasshopper be burden":

B. This refers to the image made by Nebuchadnezzar: "Nebuchadnezzar the king made an image of gold, the height of which was threescore cubits and the breadth six cubits" (Dan. 3:1).

C. Said R. Yohanan, "Any object which is sixty cubits high but only six cubits broad — can it stand? If it is not at least a third of its height in breadth it cannot stand.

D. "Yet it says, 'he set it up in the plain of Dura' (Dan. 3:1)."

E. Said R. Levi, "They set it up like a reed and it fell, and they set it up again and it fell."

F. How long?

G. R. Haggai in the name of R. Isaac said, "Until they brought all the silver and gold that they had taken from Egypt and poured it out as a base at the foot: 'They shall cast their silver in the streets and their gold shall be as an unclean thing' (Ez. 7:19)."

26. A. "and the caper bush may bud again":

B. this refers to the merit of the patriarchs.

27. A. "but man sets out for his eternal abode":

B. From Babylonia they came, and they went back there.

28. A. "with mourners all around in the street":

B. This refers to the Exile of Jeconiah.

29. A. You find that when Nebuchadnezzar went down from Jerusalem, with the exile of Zedekiah in hand, the exilic group of Jeconiah came forth to meet him, with black beneath but white outside, praising the emperor, "You have conquered barbarians!"

B. And they went about asking what had happened to father, what has happened by my brother, what has happened to my children?

C. They answered, "Those that are destined for death to death, those that are destined to the sword to the sword" (Jer. 15:2).

D. So they gave praise on the one hand and lamented on the other.

E. This fulfilled the verse: "Your head coverings shall be upon your heads, and your shoes upon your feet, you shall not make lamentation nor weep" (Ez. 24:23).

30. A. "Before the silver cord snaps":
    B. this refers to the chain of genealogy.
31. A. "and the golden bowl crashes":
    B. this refers to teachings of the Torah:
    C. "more to be desired than gold, yes, than much fine gold" (Ps. 19:11).
32. A. "the jar is shattered at the spring":
    B. Two Amoraic masters:
    C. One said, "This refers to the jar of Baruch at the fountain of Jeremiah."
    D. The other said, "This refers to the jar of Jeremiah at the foundation of Baruch."
    E. That is in line with this verse: "He pronounced all these words to me with his mouth" (Jer. 36:18).
33. A. "and the jug is smashed at the cistern":
    B. This refers to Babylonia,
    C. which is [Cohen, p. 36:] the depository of the world.

    34. A. Said R. Yohanan, "'That says to the deep, Be dry' (Is. 44:27).
        B. "Why is it called 'the deep'?
        C. "For there the waters of the Flood sank in: 'As Babylon has caused the slain of Israel to fall, so at Babylon shall fall the slain of all the land' (Jer. 51:49)."
    35. A. Said R. Simeon b. Laqish, "'They found a plain in the land of Shinar and dwelt there' (Gen. 11:2).
        B. "Why is it called Shinar?
        C. "Because the generation of the Flood were emptied out there [with the word for 'emptied out' using the consonants that appear also in the name Shinar]."
    36. A. Another explanation of the word Shinar:
        B. "They were emptied of all the commandments, the commandment of setting apart the priestly offerings and tithes."
    37. A. Another explanation of the word Shinar:
        B. The inhabitants die of suffocation, without a lamp burning, without the body's being washed.

38. A. Another explanation of the word Shinar:
    B. The inhabitants die young.
39. A. Another explanation of the word Shinar:
    B. a city whose princes are young, who trample on the Torah.
40. A. Another explanation of the word Shinar:
    B. it raised up one who hated and an enemy of the Holy One, blessed be he, namely, Nebuchadnezzar.
42. A. "and the dust returns to the ground as it was":
    B. from Babylonia they came, there they returned.
43. A. "and the lifebreath returns to God who bestowed it":
    B. this refers to the Holy Spirit.
    C. Once it had departed from them, they went into exile.
44. A. When they went into exile,
    B. Jeremiah began to lament for them: "Alas! Lonely sits the city once great with people!" (Lam. 1:1).

The systematic exposition of the intersecting verse follows a fixed form: citation of a phrase or a clause, with a brief exposition of the pertinent application to the destruction of the Temple. What is impressive is the reading of the aged king's reflections upon old age as a metaphor for the events of the destruction of the first Temple. The insertions of secondary amplifications, interpolations of various sorts, and the like scarcely confuses the matter, since the basic form is so well established and consistent throughout. The important interpolations are Nos. 20–23, 34–40, all of which violate the redactional form used here and clearly belong somewhere else; they also develop and amplify other verses than ours. So the clear intention, which is to compare the individual's old age with the nation's, is fully achieved.

4

Petihta Twenty-Four

The Valley of Vision Pronouncement. What can have happened to you that you have gone, all of you, up on the roofs, O you who were full of tumult, you clamorous town, you city so gay? Your slain are not the slain of the sword, nor the dead of battle. Your officers have all departed; they fled far away; your survivors were all taken captive, taken captive without their bows. That is why I say, "Let me be, I will weep bitterly. Press not to comfort me for the ruin of my poor people."

From Solomon's lament for his old age, now formed into a sigh for the condition of Israel, we proceed to Isaiah's Pronouncement of the Valley of Vision, which speaks of Israel in the time of the siege of Jerusalem by the Assyrians. Here is an obvious candidate for reading in light of the later siege of Jerusalem by the Babylonians, of which Jeremiah speaks in Lamentations.

XXIV.i.

1. A. R. Yohanan commenced [by citing the following verse of scripture]: " 'The Valley of Vision Pronouncement' — ["The Valley of Vision Pronouncement. What can have happened to you that you have gone, all of you, up on the roofs, O you who were full of tumult, you clamorous town, you city so gay? Your slain are not the slain of the sword, nor the dead of battle. Your officers have all departed; they fled far away; your survivors were all taken captive, taken captive without their bows. That is why I say, "Let me be, I will weep bitterly. Press not to comfort me for the ruin of my poor people." For my Lord God of Hosts had a day of tumult and din and confusion — Kir raged in the Valley of Vision, and Shoa on the hill; while Elam bore the quiver in troops of mounted men, and Kir bared the shield — and your choicest lowlands were filled with chariots and horsemen; they stormed at Judah's gateway and pressed beyond its screen. You gave thought on that day to the arms in the Forest House, and you took note of the many breaches in the city of David. And you collected the water of the Lower Pool; and you counted the Hosts of Jerusalem and pulled Hosts down to fortify the wall; and you constructed a basin between the two walls for the water of the old pool. But you gave no thought to him who planned it, you took no note of him who designed it long before. My Lord God of Hosts summoned on that day to weeping and lamenting, to tonsuring and girding with sackcloth. Instead there was rejoicing and merriment, killing of cattle and slaughtering of sheep, eating of meat and drinking of wine: "eat and drink for tomorrow we die!" Then the Lord of Hosts revealed himself to my ears: ' "This iniquity shall never be forgiven you until you die," said my Lord God of Hosts (Is. 22:1–14):]

   B. "It is a valley concerning which all seers have prophesied,

   C. "a valley from which all seers originate."

   D. For said R. Yohanan, "Every prophet the name of whose city of origin is not made explicit is a Jerusalemite."

2. A. "The Valley of Vision Pronouncement":
   B. For the words of seers were thrown to the ground there.
3. A. "What can have happened to you that you have gone, all of you, up on the roofs":
   B. But had they actually gone up to the roofs?
   C. Said R. Levi, "This refers to the arrogant ones."
4. A. "O you who were full of tumult":
   B. Said R. Eleazar b. Jacob, "The word for 'tumult' bears [Cohen, p. 37] three senses: troubles, disorders, and darkness.
   C. "'troubles': 'Neither does he hear the troubles caused by the taskmaster' (Job 39:7).
   D. "'disorders': 'You that are full of tumult.'
   E. "'darkness': 'The gloom of waste and desolation' (Is. 30:3).
5. A. "you clamorous town":
   B. city in an uproar.
6. A. "you city so gay":
   B. city rejoicing.
7. A. "Your slain are not the slain of the sword nor the dead of battle":
   B. And what are they then?
   C. "...the wasting of hunger and the devouring of the fiery bolt" (Dt. 32:24).
8. A. "Your officers have all departed, [they fled far away, your survivors were all taken captive,] taken captive without their bows":
   B. for they loosened the strings of their bows and tied them together with them.
9. A. "they fled far away, your survivors were all taken captive":
   B. they went far away from obeying the words of the Torah,
   C. in line with this verse: "From afar the Lord appeared to me" (Jer. 31:3).
10. A. "That is why I say, 'Let me be, I will weep bitterly. Press not to comfort me [for the ruin of my poor people]'":
    B. Said R. Simeon b. Laqish, "On three occasions the ministering angels wanted to recite a song before the Holy

One, blessed be he, but he did not allow them to do so, and these are they:

C. "at the generation of the flood, at the sea, and at the destruction of the house of the sanctuary.

D. "at the generation of the flood: 'And the Lord said, My spirit shall not abide in man for ever' (Gen. 6:3. [Cohen, p. 38, n. 2: *Yadon*, 'abide,' is read as *yaron*, 'sing,' and the word 'spirit' is applied to God's messengers.]

E. "at the sea: 'And the one came not near the other all the night' (Ex. 14:20).

F. "and at the destruction of the house of the sanctuary: 'That is why I say, "Let me be, I will weep bitterly. Press not to comfort me [for the ruin of my poor people]."'

G. "What is written is not, 'do not gather together,' but 'do not press.'

H. "Said the Holy One, blessed be he, to the ministering angels, 'As to these words of comfort that you recite before me, they are pressure on me.'

I. "Why so? 'For my Lord God of Hosts had a day of tumult and din and confusion.'

J. "It is a day of confusion, of plundering, of weeping."

11. A. "Kir raged in the Valley of Vision":

B. "It is a valley concerning which all seers have prophesied."

12. A. "Kir raged [in the Valley of Vision] and Shoa on the hill":

B. they demolished the walls of their Hosts, made them into barricades, and set them upon their strongholds [Cohen, p. 38].

13. A. "while Elam bore the quiver":

B. Rab said, "'a a container for arrows.'"

14. A. "in troops of mounted men, and Kir bared the shield":

B. they demolished the walls of their Hosts, made them into barricades, and set them upon their strongholds [Cohen, p. 38].

15. A. "and your choicest lowlands were filled with chariots and horsemen":

B. Rab said, "It was filled as deep as the ocean."

16. A. "they stormed at Judah's gateway":

B. [Cohen, p. 38:] troops watering their horses went, and troops watering their horses came, so that they appeared to be very numerous.

17. A. "and pressed beyond its screen":

B. they revealed what was hidden.

18. A. "You gave thought on that day to the arms in the Forest House":

B. Taught R. Simeon b. Yohai, "The Israelites had weapons at Sinai, on which the Ineffable Name of God was incised, but when they sinned, that was removed from them.

C. "'And the children of Israel were stripped of their ornament from Mount Horeb onward' (Ex. 33:6)."

D. How was it taken away from them?

E. R. Aibu and rabbis:

F. R. Aibu said, "It peeled off on its own."

G. Rabbis say, "An angel descended and peeled it off."

19. A. "you took note of the many breaches in the city of David. And you collected the water of the Lower Pool; and you counted the Hosts of Jerusalem and pulled Hosts down to fortify the wall; [and you constructed a basin between the two walls for the water of the old pool. But you gave no thought to him who planned it, you took no note of him who designed it long before]":

B. This teaches that they were tearing down their Hosts and added to the wall.

C. But had Hezekiah not done this already?

D. Is it not written, "And he took courage and built up all the wall that was broken down" (2 Chr. 32:5)?

E. "Hezekiah trusted in the Lord, God of Israel, but you did not trust in him:

F. "'But you gave no thought to him who planned it, you took no note of him who designed it long before.'"

20. A. "My Lord God of Hosts summoned on that day to weeping and lamenting, [to tonsuring and girding with sackcloth]":

B. Said the ministering angels before him, "Lord of the world, it is written, 'Honor and majesty are before him' (1 Chr. 16:27), and yet do you speak in this manner?'"

C. He said to them, "I will teach you. This is in line with the following verse: 'Strip yourselves naked, put the cloth about your loins! [Lament upon the breasts for the pleasant fields, for the spreading grapevines, for my people's soil — it shall be overgrown with briers and thistles — yes and for all the Hosts of delight, for the city of mirth]' (Is. 32:11–13).

D. "So will you be lamenting.

E. "'Lament upon the breasts': for the destruction of the first Temple and for the destruction of the second.

F. "'for the pleasant fields': for my desirable house, which I have turned into a barren field: 'Zion shall be ploughed as a field' (Mic. 3:12).

G. "'for the spreading grapevines': this refers to Israel: 'You did pluck up a vine out of Egypt' (Ps. 80:9)."

We now proceed to a sequence of further interpretations of the same clause, "My Lord God of Hosts...." These will enrich the context in which that clause is read.

21. A. Another interpretation of the passage, "My Lord God of Hosts summoned on that day to weeping and lamenting, to tonsuring and girding with sackcloth":

B. This is in line with what scripture has said through the Holy Spirit through the sons of Korah: "These things I remember and pour out my soul within me" (Ps. 42:5).

C. In regard to whom did the sons of Korah recite this verse? Did they not recite it with regard to the community of Israel?

D. For the community of Israel said before the Holy One, blessed be he, "Lord of the world, I remember full well the security and peace and prosperity in which I dwelt, but which now are far from me, so I weep and sigh, saying,

'Would that it were like those old times, when the Temple was standing, and in it you would descend from the heavens on high and bring to dwell your presence upon me.' And the nations of the world would praise me. And when I asked mercy for my sins, you would respond to me.

E. "But now I am shamed and humiliated."

F. And further did the community of Israel say before him, "Lord of the world, My soul is cast down within me when I pass by your house, which is in ruins, and a still voice in it echoes, 'In the place in which the children of Abraham would offer sacrifices before you, with the priests standing on the platform, the Levites singing praises on harps, foxes now run around.

G. "'For the mountain of Zion, which is desolate, the foxes walk upon it' (Lam. 5:18).

H. "But what can I now do, for my sins have made this happen to me, and deceitful prophets who were in my midst misled me from the way of life to the way of death."

I. That is the meaning of the verse, "These things I remember and pour out my soul within me" (Ps. 42:5).

XXIV.ii.

1. A. Another interpretation of the passage, "My Lord God of Hosts summoned on that day to weeping and lamenting, to tonsuring and girding with sackcloth":

What follows is not an interpretation of the passage, but a narrative in which the sentence of Isaiah figures. But the narrative takes over and tells the story of the conduct of God on "that day" of "weeping and lamenting."

B. When the Holy One, blessed be he, considered destroying the house of the sanctuary, he said, "So long as I am within it, the nations of the world cannot lay a hand on it.

C. "I shall close my eyes to it and take an oath that I shall not become engaged with it until the time of the end."

D. Then the enemies came and destroyed it.

E. Forthwith the Holy One, blessed be he, took an oath by his right hand and put it behind him: "He has drawn back his right hand from before the enemy" (Lam. 2:3).

F. At that moment the enemies entered the sanctuary and burned it up.

G. When it had burned, the Holy One, blessed be he, said, "I do not have any dwelling on earth any more. I shall take up my presence from there and go up to my earlier dwelling."

H. That is in line with this verse: "I will go and return to my place, until they acknowledge their guilt and seek my face" (Hos. 5:15).

I. At that moment the Holy One, blessed be he, wept, saying, "Woe is me! What have I done! I have brought my Presence to dwell below on account of the Israelites, and now that they have sinned, I have gone back to my earlier dwelling. Heaven forfend that I now become a joke to the nations and a source of ridicule among people."

J. At that moment Metatron came, prostrated himself, and said before him, "Lord of the world, let me weep, but don't you weep!"

K. He said to him, "If you do not let me weep now, I shall retreat to a place in which you have no right to enter, and there I shall weep."

L. That is in line with this verse: "But if you will not hear it, my soul shall weep in secret for pride" (Jer. 13:17).

2. A. Said the Holy One, blessed be he, to the ministering angels, "Let's go and see what the enemies have done to my house."

B. Forthwith the Holy One, blessed be he, and the ministering angels went forth, with Jeremiah before them.

C. When the Holy One, blessed be he, saw the house of the sanctuary, he said, "This is certainly my house, and this is my resting place, and the enemies have come and done whatever they pleased with it!"

D. At that moment the Holy One, blessed be he, wept, saying "Woe is me for my house! O children of mine —

where are you? O priests of mine — where are you? O you who love me — where are you? What shall I do for you? I warned you, but you did not repent."

E. Said the Holy One, blessed be he, to Jeremiah, "Today I am like a man who had an only son, who made a marriage canopy for him, and the son died under his marriage canopy. Should you not feel pain for me and for my son?

F. "Go and call Abraham, Isaac, Jacob, and Moses from their graves, for they know how to weep."

G. He said before him, "Lord of the world, I don't know where Moses is buried."

H. The Holy One, blessed be he, said to him, "Go and stand at the bank of the Jordan and raise your voice and call him, 'Son of Amram, son of Amram, rise up and see your flock, which the enemy has swallowed up!'"

I. Jeremiah immediately went to the cave of Machpelah and said to the founders of the world, "Arise, for the time has come for you to be called before the Holy One, blessed be he."

J. They said to him, "Why?"

K. He said to them, "I don't know," because he was afraid that they would say to him, "In your time this has come upon our children!"

L. Jeremiah left them and went to the bank of the Jordan and cried out, "Son of Amram, son of Amram, rise up, for the time has come for you to be called before the Holy One, blessed be he."

M. He said to him, "What makes this day so special, that I am called before the Holy One, blessed be he?"

N. He said to them, "I don't know."

O. Moses left him and went to the ministering angels, for he had known them from the time of the giving of the Torah. He said to them, "You who serve on high! Do you know on what account I am summoned before the Holy One, blessed be he?"

P. They said to him, "Son of Amram! Don't you know that the house of the sanctuary has been destroyed, and the Israelites taken away into exile?"

Q. So he cried and wept until he came to the fathers of the world. They too forthwith tore their garments and put their hands on their heads, crying and weeping, up to the gates of the house of the sanctuary.

R. When the Holy One, blessed be he, saw them, forthwith: "My Lord God of Hosts summoned on that day to weeping and lamenting, to tonsuring and girding with sackcloth."

S. Were it not stated explicitly in a verse of scripture, it would not be possible to make this statement.

T. And they went weeping from this gate to that, like a man whose deceased lies before him,

U. and the Holy One, blessed be he, wept, lamenting, "Woe for a king who prospers in his youth and not in his old age."

Solomon, we recall, wept for the Temple that he built. Now God laments for the aged king and his works. In what follows, the story moves along, with God confronting the reproach of the patriarchs.

3. A. Said R. Samuel bar Nahman, "When the Temple was destroyed, Abraham came before the Holy One, blessed be he, weeping, pulling at his beard and tearing his hair, striking his face, tearing his clothes, with ashes on his head, walking about the Temple, weeping and crying, saying before the Holy One, blessed be he,

B. "'How come I am treated differently from every other nation and language, that I should be brought to such humiliation and shame!'

C. "When the ministering angels saw him, they too [Cohen, p. 43:] composed lamentations, arranging themselves in rows, saying,

D. "'the highways lie waste, the wayfaring man ceases' (Is. 33:8)."

E. "What is the meaning of the statement, 'the highways lie waste'?

F. "Said the ministering angels before the Holy One, blessed be he, 'The highways that you paved to Jerusalem, so that the wayfarers would not cease, how have they become a desolation?'

G. "'the wayfaring man ceases':

H. "Said the ministering angels before the Holy One, blessed be he, 'How have the ways become deserted, on which the Israelites would come and go for the pilgrim festivals?'

I. "'You have broken the covenant':

J. "Said the ministering angels before the Holy One, blessed be he, 'Lord of the world, the covenant that was made with their father, Abraham, has been broken, the one through which the world was settled and through which you were made known in the world, that you are the most high God, the one who possesses heaven and earth.'

K. "'He has despised the cities':

L. "Said the ministering angels before the Holy One, blessed be he, 'You have despised Jerusalem and Zion after you have chosen them!'"

M. "Thus scripture says, 'Have you utterly rejected Judah? Has your soul loathed Zion?' (Jer. 14:19).

N. "'He regards not Enosh':

O. "Said the ministering angels before the Holy One, blessed be he, 'Even as much as the generation of Enosh, chief of all idol worshippers, you have not valued Israel!'

P. "At that moment the Holy One, blessed be he, responded to the ministering angels, saying to them, 'How come you composing lamentations, arranging yourselves in rows, on this account?'

Q. "They said to him, 'Lord of the world! It is on account of Abraham, who loved you, who came to your house and lamented and wept. How come you didn't pay any attention to him?'

R. "He said to them, 'From the day on which my beloved died, going off to his eternal house, he has not come to my house, and now "what is my beloved doing in my house" (Jer. 11:15)?"

S. "Said Abraham before the Holy One, blessed be he, 'Lord of the world! How come you have sent my children into exile and handed them over to the nations? And they have killed them with all manner of disgusting forms of death! And you have destroyed the house of the sanctuary, the place on which I offered up my son Isaac as a burnt-offering before you!?'

T. "Said to Abraham the Holy One, blessed be he, 'Your children sinned and violated the whole Torah, transgressing the twenty-two letters that are used to write it: "Yes, all Israel have transgressed your Torah" (Dan. 9:11).'

U. "Said Abraham before the Holy One, blessed be he, 'Lord of the world, who will give testimony against the Israelites, that they have violated your Torah?'

V. "He said to him, 'Let the Torah come and give testimony against the Israelites.'

W. "Forthwith the Torah came to give testimony against them.

X. "Said Abraham to her, 'My daughter, have you come to give testimony against the Israelites that they have violated your religious duties? And are you not ashamed on my account? Remember the day on which the Holy One, blessed be he, peddled you to all the nations and languages of the world, and no one wanted to accept you, until my children came to Mount Sinai and they accepted you and honored you! And now are you coming to give testimony against them on their day of disaster?'

Y. "When the Torah heard this, she went off to one side and did not testify against them.

Z. "Said the Holy One, blessed be he, to Abraham, 'Then let the twenty-two letters of the alphabet come and give testimony against the Israelites.'

AA. "Forthwith the twenty-two letters of the alphabet came to give testimony against them.

BB. "The aleph came to give testimony against the Israelites, that they had violated the Torah.

CC. "Said Abraham to her, 'Aleph, you are the head of all of the letters of the alphabet, and have you now come to give testimony against the Israelites on the day of their disaster?'

DD. "'Remember the day on which the Holy One, blessed be he, revealed himself on Mount Sinai and began his discourse with you: "I [anokhi, beginning with aleph] am the Lord your God who brought you out of the Land of Egypt, out of the house of bondage" (Ex. 20:2).

EE. "'But not a single nation or language was willing to take you on, except for my children! And are you now going to give testimony against my children?'

FF. "Forthwith the aleph went off to one side and did not testify against them.

GG. "The bet came to give testimony against the Israelites.

HH. "Said Abraham to her, 'My daughter, have you come to give testimony against my children, who are meticulous about the Five Books of the Torah, at the head of which you stand, as it is said, "In the beginning [bereshit] God created..." (Gen. 1:1)?'

II. "Forthwith the bet went off to one side and did not testify against them.

JJ. "The gimel came to give testimony against the Israelites.

KK. "Said Abraham to her, 'Gimel, have you come to give testimony against my children, that they have violated the Torah? Is there any nation, besides my children, that carries out the religious duty of wearing show-fringes, at the head of which you stand, as it is said, "Twisted cords [gedelim] you shall make for yourself" (Dt. 22:12).'

LL. "Forthwith the gimel went off to one said and did not testify against them.

MM. "Now when all of the letters of the alphabet realized that Abraham had silenced them, they were ashamed and stood off and would not testify against Israel.

NN. "Abraham forthwith commenced speaking before the Holy One, blessed be he, saying to him, 'Lord of the world, when I was a hundred years old, you gave me a son. And when he had already reached the age of volition, a boy thirty-seven years of age, you told me, "offer him up as a burnt-offering before me"!

OO. " 'And I turned mean to him and had no mercy for him, but I myself tied him up. Are you not going to remember this and have mercy on my children?'

PP. "Isaac forthwith commenced speaking before the Holy One, blessed be he, saying to him, 'Lord of the world, when father said to me, "God will see to the lamb for the offering for himself, my son" (Gen. 22:8), I did not object to what you had said, but I was bound willingly, with all my heart, on the altar, and spread forth my neck under the knife. Are you not going to remember this and have mercy on my children?'

QQ. "Jacob forthwith commenced speaking before the Holy One, blessed be he, saying to him, 'Lord of the world, did I not remain in the house of Laban for twenty years? And when I went forth from his house, the wicked Esau met me and wanted to kill my children, and I gave myself over to death in their behalf. Now my children are handed over to their enemies like sheep for slaughter, after I raised them like fledglings of chickens. I bore on their account the anguish of raising children, for through most of my life I was pained greatly on their account. And now are you not going to remember this and have mercy on my children?'

RR. "Moses forthwith commenced speaking before the Holy One, blessed be he, saying to him, 'Lord of the world, was I not a faithful shepherd for the Israelites for forty years? I ran before them in the desert like a horse. And when the time came for them to enter the land, you issued a decree against me in the wilderness that there my bones would fall. And now that they have gone into exile, you have sent to me to mourn and weep for them.'

SS. "This is in line with the proverb people say: 'When it's good for my master, it's not good for me, but when its bad for him, it's bad for me!'

TT. "Then Moses said to Jeremiah, 'Go before me, so I may go and bring them in and see who will lay a hand on them.'

UU. "Said to him Jeremiah, 'It isn't even possible to go along the road, because of the corpses.'

VV. "He said to him, 'Nonetheless.'

WW. "Forthwith Moses went along, with Jeremiah leading the way, until they came to the waters of Babylon.

XX. "They saw Moses and said to one another, 'Here comes the son of Amram from his grave to redeem us from the hand of our oppressors.'

YY. "An echo went forth and said, 'It is a decree from before me.'

ZZ. "Then said Moses to them, 'My children, to bring you back is not possible, for the decree has already been issued. But the Omnipresent will bring you back quickly.' Then he left them.

AAA. "Then they raised up their voices in weeping until the sound rose on high: 'By the rivers of Babylon there we sat down, yes, we wept' (Ps. 137:1).

BBB. "When Moses got back to the fathers of the world, they said to him, 'What have the enemies done to our children?'

CCC. "He said to them, 'Some of them he killed, the hands of some of them he bound behind their backs, some of them he put in iron chains, some of them he stripped naked, some of them died on the way, and their corpses were left for the vultures of heaven and the hyenas of the earth, some of them were left for the sun, starving and thirsting.'

DDD. "Then they began to weep and sing dirges: 'Woe for what has happened to our children! How have you become orphans without a father! How have you had to sleep in the hot sun during the summer without clothes and covers! How have you had to walk over rocks and stones without shoes and sandals! How were you burdened with heavy

bundles of sand! How were your hands bound behind
your backs! How were you left unable even to swallow
the spit in your mouths!'

EEE. "Moses then said, 'Cursed are you, O sun! Why did you
not grow dark when the enemy went into the house of
the sanctuary?'

FFF. "The sun answered him, 'By your life, Moses, faithful
shepherd! They would not let me nor did they leave me
alone, but beat me with sixty whips of fire, saying, "Go,
pour out your light."'

GGG. "Moses then said, 'Woe for your brilliance, O Temple,
how has it become darkened? Woe that its time has come
to be destroyed, for the building to be reduced to ruins,
for the school children to be killed, for their parents to go
into captivity and exile and the sword!'

HHH. "Moses then said, 'O you who have taken the captives!
I impose an oath on you by your lives! If you kill, do
not kill with a cruel form of death, do not exterminate
them utterly, do not kill a son before his father, a daughter
before her mother, for the time will come for the Lord of
heaven to exact a full reckoning from you!'

III. "The wicked Chaldeans did not do things this way, but
they brought a son before his mother and said to the father, 'Go, kill him!' The mother wept, her tears flowing
over him, and the father hung his head.

JJJ. "And further Moses said before him, 'Lord of the world!
You have written in your Torah, "Whether it is a cow or
a ewe, you shall not kill it and its young both in one day"
(Lev. 22:28).

KKK. "'But have they not killed any number of children along
with their mothers, and yet you remain silent!'

LLL. "Then Rachel, our mother, leapt to the fray and said to
the Holy One, blessed be he, 'Lord of the world! It is perfectly self-evident to you that your servant, Jacob, loved
me with a mighty love, and worked for me for father
for seven years, but when those seven years were fulfilled,
and the time came for my wedding to my husband, father

planned to substitute my sister for me in the marriage to my husband. Now that matter was very hard for me, for I knew the deceit, and I told my husband and gave him a sign by which he would know the difference between me and my sister, so that my father would not be able to trade me off. But then I regretted it and I bore my passion, and I had mercy for my sister, that she should not be shamed. So in the evening for my husband they substituted my sister for me, and I gave my sister all the signs that I had given to my husband, so that he would think that she was Rachel.

MMM. " 'And not only so, but I crawled under the bed on which he was lying with my sister, while she remained silent, and I made all the replies so that he would not discern the voice of my sister.

NNN. " 'I paid my sister only kindness, and I was not jealous of her, and I did not allow her to be shamed, and I am a mere mortal, dust and ashes. Now I had no envy of my rival, and I did not place her at risk for shame and humiliation. But you are the King, living and enduring and merciful. How come then you are jealous of idolatry, which is nothing, and so have sent my children into exile, allowed them to be killed by the sword, permitted the enemy to do whatever they wanted to them?!'

OOO. "Forthwith the mercy of the Holy One, blessed be he, welled up, and he said, 'For Rachel I am going to bring the Israelites back to their land.'

PPP. "That is in line with this verse of scripture: 'Thus said the Lord: A cry is heard in Ramah, wailing, bitter weeping, Rachel weeping for her children. She refuses to be comforted for her children, who are gone. Thus said the Lord, Restrain your voice from weeping, your eyes from shedding tears; for there is a reward for your labor, declares the Lord; they shall return from the enemy's land, and there is hope for your future, declares the Lord: your children shall return to their country' " (Jer. 31:15–17).

This wonderful passage is made up of two completely separate entries, one following the familiar form of a clause-by-clause amplification of a verse of scripture, the other a completely different kind of writing altogether. XXIV.i.1–21 yields a fairly well disciplined statement on the intersecting verse cited at the head; there is no base verse that I can identify. Perhaps at some point Lamentations 5:18 was conceived to serve as the base verse, but that is hardly obvious. XXIV.ii.1 is tacked on because of the amplification of the same verse that forms the basis of the concluding unit of the foregoing. But we must regard the whole as an essentially fresh statement. I have divided the whole into three parts, since Samuel bar Nahman's massive essay clearly stands wholly on its own. It seems to me beyond reasonable doubt that the whole of XXIV.ii.3 forms a unitary and well-crafted composition, with no important interpolations or imperfections of any kind. I also see XXIV.ii.1 as essentially autonomous. But one can make the point that No. 2 continues No. 1, and I cannot make a strong case for my division. The link between No. 3 and No. 2 is via the patriarchs and Moses, and so the whole is, if divided, still quite cogent. I cannot point in Midrash compilations that reached closure prior to this one to a passage of the narrative ambition and power of Samuel bar Nahman's. We are in a completely different literary situation when we come to so long and so carefully formed a story as this one.

5

Parashah I
Lamentations 1:3

Judah has gone into exile
because of affliction and hard servitude;
she dwells now among the nations,
but finds no resting place;
her pursuers have all overtaken her
in the midst of her distress.

From the set of prologues, which convey the mood and lesson of the book as a whole, we proceed to a phrase-by-phrase reading of verses of Lamentations itself. Here we raise a reasonable question: why should the Israelites make such a to-do about their exile, when going into exile is commonplace in the world. What differentiates the Israelites from all other nations that exile should weigh so heavily upon them?

XXXVII.i.
1. A. "Judah has gone into exile":
   B. Do not the nations of the world go into exile?

44

C. Even though they go into exile, their exile is not really an exile at all.

D. But for Israel, their exile really is an exile.

E. The nations of the world, who eat the bread and drink the wine of others, do not really experience exile.

F. But the Israelites, who do not eat the bread and drink the wine of others, really do experience exile.

G. The nations of the world, who [Cohen, p. 96:] travel in litters, do not really experience exile.

H. But the Israelites, who [in poverty] go barefoot — their exile really is an exile.

I. That is why it is said, "Judah has gone into exile."

We now read the same clause in a different way, comparing its language to that of parallel passages and drawing conclusions from the difference.

2. A. Here scripture states, "Judah has gone into exile,"

B. and elsewhere, "So Judah was carried away captive out of his land" (Jer. 52:27).

C. When they went into exile, they grew weak like a woman,

D. so it is said, "Judah has gone into exile."

The next clause raises a philological question, which our sages answer by looking for meanings assigned to the same word in other contexts, a perfectly natural procedure. But this permits our sages to tote up the sins that the Israelites have committed, thus bringing upon themselves the disaster.

3. A. "because of affliction [and hard servitude]":

B. [Interpreting the word "affliction" by reference to other words that are formed of the same consonants:] because they ate leaven on Passover:

C. "You shall eat no leavened bread with it; seven days you shall eat unleavened bread with it, even the bread of affliction" (Dt. 16:3).

4. A. Another interpretation of the phrase, "because of affliction [and hard servitude]":

   B. because they took the pledge of a poor inside of their houses:

   C. "And if he is poor, you shall not sleep with his pledge" (Dt. 24:12).

5. A. Another interpretation of the phrase, "because of affliction [and hard servitude]":

   B. because they withheld the wages of a hired servant:

   C. "You shall not afflict a hired servant who is poor and needy" (Dt. 24:14).

6. A. Another interpretation of the phrase, "because of affliction [and hard servitude]":

   B. because they ate the tithe that belonged to the poor.

   C. R. Bibi and R. Huna in the name of Rab: "He who eats produce subject to tithes from which the poor man's tithe has not been removed is subject to the death penalty."

7. A. Another interpretation of the phrase, "because of affliction [and hard servitude]":

   B. because of idolatry:

   C. "But the noise of them who sing do I hear" (Ex. 32:18).

   D. R. Aha said, "Because of the sound of praise of idolatry do I hear."

   E. R. Judah in the name of R. Yosé, "No generation passes that is not punished in some way for the sin of the golden calf."

8. A. "and hard servitude":

   B. R. Aha said, "Because they kept in servitude the Hebrew slave:

   C. "'At the end of seven years you shall let go every man his brother who is a Hebrew slave'" (Jer. 34:14).

We have a fine phrase-by-phrase clarification of part of our base verse, with an excellent inquiry into the intersections between verses that use a word with the same consonants as appears in our base verse. The message is a cogent one, carried out in details: Israel has brought upon itself the destruction that it now laments. We proceed to the next clauses.

XXXVII.ii.

1.A. "she dwells now among the nations, but finds no resting place":

B. R. Yudan b. R. Nehemiah in the name of R. Simeon b. Laqish said, "Had [Israel] found rest, she would not have returned.

C. "Along these same lines: 'But the dove found no rest for the sole of her foot, and she returned to him to the ark' (Gen. 8:9).

D. "'And among the nations you shall have no repose, and there shall be no rest for the sole of your foot' (Dt. 28:65)."

2.A. "her pursuers have all overtaken her in the midst of her distress":

B. That is in line with that which we have learned in the Mishnah:

C. These are the words of Ben Nannos, "Within its marks and boundaries" [M. B. B. 7:3E]. [Cohen, p. 98, n. 1: The word "distress" is explained as equal to the technical term "boundaries" in the cited passage.]

3.A. Another interpretation of the phrase, "her pursuers have all overtaken her in the midst of her distress":

B. ["In the midst of her distress" means,] in the days of distress between the seventeenth of Tammuz and the ninth of Ab, when the demon of pestilence is prevalent: "Of the pestilence that walks in darkness" (Dt. 91:6).

C. R. Abba bar Kahana and R. Levi:

D. R. Abba bar Kahana said, "That demon walks about during the midday, from the beginning of the sixth hour to the end of the ninth hour."

E. R. Levi said, "That demon [Cohen, p. 98:] spoils the course of the day from the end of the fourth hour until the beginning of the ninth, and it does not walk in the sun or shade but in the shadow near the sun."

F. R. Yohanan and R. Simeon b. Laqish:

G. R. Yohanan said, "[Cohen, p. 99:] It is all over full of eyes, scales, and hair."

H. R. Simeon b. Laqish, "[Cohen, p. 99:] It has one eye set over its heart, and whoever looks at it falls down dead."

I. There is the case of a pious man who looked at it and fell down dead.

J. Some say R. Judah b. Rabbi was the one.

K. Samuel looked at it but did not fall down, and nonetheless he did die.

4. A. R. Abbahu was in session at the synagogue in Caesarea, and there was a man carrying a stick, who was planning to hit his fellow, but that particular demon was standing behind him with an iron rod.

B. R. Abbahu went and restrained him, saying, "Do you want to kill your fellow?"

C. The man said to him, "Can someone kill his fellow with a stick like this?"

D. He said to him, "That demon was standing behind you carrying a rod of iron. You will hit the man with this stick, and he will hit him with the other, and the man will die."

5. A. R. Yohanan would instruct the teachers for elementary matters and the Mishnah during the specified days [the seventeenth of Tammuz through the ninth of Ab] not to hit the students with a strap.

B. R. Samuel b. Nahman would instruct the teachers for elementary matters and the Mishnah during the specified hours not to dismiss the children.

The clarification of the base verse proceeds apace at No. 1. No. 2 appeals to a language usage to interpret the specified word. No. 3 goes on to identify the days of distress with the period between the first fast day in observance of the destruction and the second. The tacked-on materials, of course, are included for thematic reasons.

6

Parashah I
Lamentations 1:5

Her foes have become the head, her enemies prosper,
because the Lord has made her suffer
for the multitude of her transgressions;
her children have gone away, captives before the foe.

Our reading of verses in Lamentations, phrase by phrase, accomplishes the goal of finding numerous details that cohere to make a single point. Here, that single point is that whoever torments Jerusalem is made the head, and a number of examples of that correlation are set forth.

XXXIX.i.
1. A. "Her foes have become the head":
    B. Said R. Hillel b. Berekhiah, "Whoever comes to torment Jerusalem is made head,
    C. "for it is written, 'Her foes have become the head.'"

D. "[Following the order of Cohen's text, p. 100:] You find that before Jerusalem was destroyed, no city was regarded as important. Afterward, Caesarea became a metropolis, Antipatris, a city, and Neapolis a colony."

2. A. Another reading of "Her foes have become the head":
   B. this refers to Nebuchadnezzar.

3. A. "Her foes have become the head":
   B. this refers to Nebuzaradan.

4. A. Another interpretation of the phrase "Her foes have become the head":
   B. this refers to Vespasian.
   C. "her enemies prosper":
   D. this refers to Titus.

The clause-by-clause explication defines the form before us. The point of interest, of course, is introducing not only the first destruction, but also the second, and that accounts for the enormous interpolation that follows.

XXXIX:ii.

1. A. For three and a half years Vespasian surrounded Jerusalem, with four generals with him: the generals of Arabia, Africa, Alexandria, and [Cohen:] Palestine.
   B. What was the name [of the general of Arabia]?
   C. Two Amoraic authorities:
   D. One said, "His name was Illam."
   E. The other said, "His name was Abgar."

2. A. In Jerusalem were three rich men, any one of whom had the resources to feed the city for five years: Ben Sisit, Ben Kalba-Shabua, and Naqdimon Ben Gurion.
   B. And there also was Ben Battiah, son of Rabban Yohanan b. Zakkai's daughter, who was in charge of the stores.
   C. He went and burned all the stores.
   D. Rabban Yohanan ben Zakkai heard and cried, "Woe!"
   E. People went and said, "Lo, your friend said, 'woe.'"
   F. He sent and summoned him, saying to him, "Why did you cry, 'woe'?"
   G. He said to him, "I did not say 'woe' but 'wow.'"
   H. He said to him, "Why did you say 'wow'?"

I. He said to him, "I was thinking that so long as the stores were available, the people of the city would not give themselves up to make sorties and do battle and engage the enemy."

J. Through the difference between "woe" and "wow," Rabban Yohanan ben Zakkai was saved.

K. This verse of scripture applies to him: "The excellency of knowledge is that wisdom preserves the life of the one who has it" (Qoh. 7:12).

3. A. Three days later Rabban Yohanan ben Zakkai went out to stroll in the market, and he saw people boiling straw and drinking the water.

B. He said, "Can people who boil straw and drink the water stand before the armies of Vespasian? The simple fact is that I have to get myself out of here."

C. Rabban Yohanan sent to Ben Battiah, "Get me out of here."

D. He said to him, "We have agreed that no one is going to get out except for a corpse."

E. He said to him, "Get me out as a corpse."

F. R. Eliezer carried him at the head, R. Joshua at the feet, and Ben Battiah walked in front. When they got to the gates, the guards wanted to stab the corpse. Ben Battiah said to them, "Do you want people to say that when our teacher died, they stabbed his body?" They let them pass.

G. When they had passed the gates, they carried him to the cemetery and left him there and went back to the city.

4. A. Rabban Yohanan b. Zakkai emerged and went among Vespasian's troops, saying to them, "Where is the king?"

B. They went and told Vespasian, "A Jew wants you."

C. He said to them, "Bring him along."

D. When he came in, he said, *"Vive domine Imperator!"*

E. Vespasian said to him, "You greet me as a king but I am not, and if the king hears, he will assassinate me."

F. He said to him, "If you are not a king, you will be, because the Temple will be destroyed only by the power of a king: 'And Lebanon shall fall by a mighty one' (Is. 10:34)."

5. A. They took [Rabban Yohanan ben Zakkai] and put him inside the innermost of seven rooms and asked him what time of night it was.

B. He told them.

C. They asked him, "What time of the day is it?"

D. He told them.

E. How did he know it?

F. From his study [he kept repeating traditions, and these told him the passage of time].

6. A. Three days later Vespasian went to wash at Gophna. After he had bathed, he came out and put on his shoes. But when he had put on one of his shoes, they brought him a writing from Rome that the king had died and the citizens of Rome had crowned him king.

B. He wanted to put on the other shoe and he could not put it on his foot.

C. He sent for Rabban Yohanan ben Zakkai and asked, "Can you tell me why all these years I have been able to put on these shoes, but when I put on one of them and wanted to put on the other, it would not go on my foot?"

D. He said to him, "You have heard good news: 'A good report makes the bones fat' (Prov. 15:30)."

E. "And what shall I do to get it on?"

F. He said to him, "If you have an enemy, or some one you owe, let him walk in front of you, and your flesh will shrink: 'A broken spirit dries bones' (Prov. 17:22)."

7. A. The generals began to speak in parables before him: "As to a cask in which a snake has nested, what is to be done with it?"

B. He said to him, "Bring a charmer and charm the snake."

C. Said Amgar [Cohen: Pangar], "Kill the snake and break the cask."

D. "If a snake nested in a tower, what is to be done with it?"

E. "Bring a charmer and charm the snake, and leave the tower be."

F. Said Amgar, "Kill the snake and burn the tower."

G. Said Rabban Yohanan ben Zakkai, "All neighbors who do injury do it to their neighbors: Instead of defending us, you argue for the prosecution against us."

H. He said to him, "By your life! It is for your benefit that I have said what I said. So long as the Temple is standing, the nations will envy you. But if it is destroyed, they will not envy you."

I. Said to him Rabban Yohanan ben Zakkai, "The heart truly knows whether it is woven or crooked [that is, what your intention really is]."

8. A. Vespasian said to Rabban Yohanan ben Zakkai, "Ask for something, and I shall give it to you."

B. He said to him, "I ask you to leave the city and go away."

C. He said to him, "The citizens of Rome did not make me king except to carry out public policy, and you tell me to leave the city and go away?! Ask something else, and I will do it."

D. He said to him, "I ask you to leave the western gate, which leads to Lydda, and spare everyone who leaves up to the fourth hour."

9. A. After he had come and conquered the city, he said to him, "If you have a relative there, send and bring him out."

B. He sent R. Eliezer and R. Joshua to bring out R. Saddoq, whom they found at the city gate.

C. When he came, Rabban Yohanan stood up before him.

D. Vespasian asked, "Are you honoring this emaciated old man?"

E. He said to him, "By your life, if in Jerusalem there had been one more like him, even though your army were twice as big, you would not have been able to take the city."

F. He said to him, "What is his power?"

G. He said to him, "He eats a single fig, and on the strength it gives him, he teaches a hundred sessions at the academy."

H. "Why is he so thin?"

I. "Because of his many abstinences and fasts."

J. Vespasian called physicians, who fed him little by little with food and drink until he recovered his strength.

K. [Saddoq's] son, Eleazar, said to him, "Father, give them their reward in this world, lest they have merit on your account in the world to come."

L. He gave them [Cohen:] calculation by fingers and scales for weighing.

10. A. When they had conquered the city, he divided the destruction of the four ramparts to the four generals, with the western one to Pangar.

B. Heaven had decreed that the western wall should never be destroyed.

C. The three other generals destroyed their parts, but he did not destroy his.

D. He sent and summoned him and said, "Why did you not destroy your part?"

E. He said to him, "If I had destroyed my part as the others destroyed theirs, the kingdoms that will arise after you would never know about the great glory of what you have destroyed. But when people look [at the western wall], they will say, 'See the power of Vespasian from what he destroyed!'"

F. He said to him, "By your life, you have spoken well. But because you have disobeyed my orders, I decree for you that you go up and throw yourself off the top of the gate. If you live, you live, if you die, you die."

G. He went up, threw himself off, and died.

H. So did the curse of Rabban Yohanan ben Zakkai stick to him.

I have tried to divide the whole into what seem to me its obviously distinct units, but, of course, others may see connections where I do not, e.g., between the four generals and the councillors in Jerusalem, Nos. 1, 2. Certainly the "three days later" materials form clearly defined units, No. 3 for instance. Cohen's version of the text marks a clear break at No. 4, and, as we have it, No. 5 is unconnected to No. 4. But the recurrent motif throughout is that the sage is saved by his sagacity, and this is made explicit, e.g., in 5.F, as well as at each point at which a proof text occurs. For example, in No. 6 the implicit polemic is that knowing the Torah yields salvation. The sage's wit is in play also in No. 7. No. 8 represents Yohanan as asking for the city's salvation, not merely for his private wants, as other stories have it. No. 9 is not prepared for, but its main point surely is needed: the sage could have saved the city. No. 10, of course, has been prepared for, and the fate of Pangar picks up a thread introduced earlier ("The heart truly knows whether it is woven or crooked"). The whole then is rather haphazard and disjointed, but the main points are clear. None of this has any close bearing upon our proof text, of course, since the climax, No. 10, makes exactly the opposite point from "her enemies prosper." Now we return to our base verse and continue to explain its elements, one by one.

XXXIX:iii.

1. A. "because the Lord has made her suffer":
   B. Did he act without reason?
   C. "for the multitude of her transgressions."
2. A. "her children have gone away, captives before the foe":
   B. Said R. Judah, "Come and notice how much the Holy One, blessed be he, loves children.
   C. "The ten tribes went into exile, but the Presence of God did not go into exile.
   D. "Judah and Benjamin went into exile, but the Presence of God did not go into exile.
   E. "The sanhedrin went into exile, but the Presence of God did not go into exile.
   F. "The priestly watches went into exile, but the Presence of God did not go into exile.
   G. "But when the children went into exile, then the Presence of God went into exile: 'her children have gone away, captives before the foe.'
   H. "And what follows immediately?
   I. "'From the daughter of Zion has departed all her majesty.'"

The clause-by-clause amplification yields, in No. 2, a particularly powerful presentation, which draws upon the juxtaposition of the cited verses to make a fresh and stunning point.

7

Parashah I
Lamentations 1:16

For these things I weep;
my eyes flow with tears;
for a comforter is far from me,
one to revive my courage;
my children are desolate, for the enemy has prevailed.

As we noted when we met the tale of Yohanan ben Zakkai and Vespasian, Lamentations Rabbah contains not only comments on verses, but also narratives that on their own treat the theme of the book rather than its wording. Certainly the most powerful story concerns not the destruction of the first Temple, but the suffering in the aftermath of the destruction of the second Temple in 70 C.E. The verse "For these things I weep" in this setting serves as a head to what is to follow: here are stories of sanctity and suffering for which I weep:

L.i.
    1. A. "For these things I weep":
       B. Vespasian — may his bones be pulverized! — filled three

ships with men and women of the nobility of Jerusalem, planning to place them in the brothels of Rome. When they had embarked on the sea, they said, "Is it not enough for us that we have angered our God in his holy house? Shall we now outrage him overseas as well?"

C. They said to the women, "Do you want such a thing?"

D. They said to them, "No."

E. They said, "Now if these, who are built for sexual relations, do not want it, as to us, how much the more so!"

F. They said to them, "Do you think that if we throw ourselves into the sea, we shall have a portion in the world to come?"

G. The Holy One, blessed be he, enlightened them with this verse: "The Lord said, I will bring them back from Bashan, I will bring them back from the depths of the sea" (Ps. 68:23).

H. "I will bring them back from Bashan": "I will bring them back from between the teeth of lions."

I. "I will bring them back from the depths of the sea": this is meant literally.

J. The first company stood up and said, "Surely we had not forgotten the name of our God or spread forth our hands to a strange God" (Ps. 44:21), and threw themselves into the sea.

K. The second company went and said, "No, but for your sake we are killed all day long" (Ps. 44:23), and they threw themselves into the sea.

L. The third company went and said, "Would not God search this out? For he knows the secrets of the heart" (Ps. 44:22), and they threw themselves into the sea.

M. And the Holy Spirit cried, "For these things I weep."

2. A. "For these things I weep":

B. Hadrian — may his bones be pulverized — set up three guards, one in Emmaus, one in Kefar Leqatia, and the third in Bethel in Judah.

C. He thought, "Whoever escapes the one will be caught by the other."

D. He sent forth a proclamation, saying, "Wherever a Jew is located, let him come out, because the king wants to assure him."

E. The heralds made this announcement and caught Jews, in line with this verse: "And Ephraim is become like a silly dove, without understanding" (Hos. 7:11).

F. [The Jews who were caught were taunted:] "Instead of asking that the dead be resurrected, pray that those alive will not be caught" [following Cohen, p. 126].

G. Those who understood did not come out of hiding, but those who did not gathered in the valley of Bet Rimmon.

H. [Hadrian] said to his general, "Before I am done eating this piece of cake and chicken leg, I want to be able to look for a single one of these yet alive and not find him."

I. He surrounded them with the legions and slaughtered them, so the blood streams as far as Cyprus.

J. And the Holy Spirit cried, "For these things I weep."

3. A. There was the case of one band that was hidden in a cave. They said to one of them, "Go out and bring us one of those who were killed," which they ate.

B. One day they said, "Let one of us go and if he finds something, let him bring it, and we shall have something to eat."

C. He went out and found his father killed, and he buried him and marked the spot.

D. He came back and said, "I found nothing."

E. Another one of them went out in the direction of that deceased and found the body and brought it back to them and they ate it.

F. Afterward they said to him, "Where did you find this corpse?"

G. He said to them, "In such and such a place."

H. "And what was the mark?"

I. He told them.

J. The other said, "Woe is me, I have eaten the flesh of my father."

K. This exemplifies the verse: "Therefore the fathers shall eat the sons in the midst of you, and the sons shall eat their fathers" (Ez. 5:10).

4. A. The wife of Trajan — may his bones be pulverized — gave birth to a child on the ninth of Ab, while the Jews were observing rites of mourning, and the child died on Hanukkah.

B. They said to one another, "What shall we do? Shall we kindle the Hanukkah lights or not?"

C. They said, "Let us light them, and what will be will be."

D. They went and slandered the Jews to him, saying to his wife, "When your son was born, these Jews went into mourning, and when he died, they lit their lamps."

E. She sent and said to her husband, "Instead of conquering the barbarians, come and conquer these Jews, who have rebelled against you.

F. He had made a calculation that the trip would take ten days, but the winds carried him and brought him in five days.

G. He came into the synagogue and found the Jews occupied with this verse of scripture: "The Lord will bring a nation against you from afar, from the end of the earth, as the vulture swoops down" (Dt. 28:49).

H. He said to them, "I am he. I thought that I would come to you in ten days, but I came in five."

I. He surrounded them with his legions and killed them.

J. He said to the women, "Submit to my legions, and if not, I shall do to you what I did to your husbands."

K. They said to him, "Then what you did to the men do to the women."

L. He surrounded them with his legions and killed them.

M. So their blood mingled with the blood of the others and streamed as far as Cyprus.

N. And the Holy Spirit cried, "For these things I weep."

5. A. There was the case of the two children of R. Saddoq, high priest, who were taken captive, one a boy, the other a girl, each falling to a different officer.

B. This one went to a whore and handed over the boy as her fee.

C. That one went to a storekeeper and handed over the girl as his fee for wine.

D. This exemplifies the verse of scripture, "And they have given a boy for a harlot and sold a girl for wine" (Joel 4:3).

E. After some days the whore went to the storekeeper and said to him, "I have a Jewish boy and he is ready for that girl you have. Let's match them up with one another, and whatever they produce as a child we can divide among us.

F. They did so. They closed them up in a room, and the girl started crying. The boy asked her, "Why are you crying?"

G. She said to him, "Woe for this daughter of the high priest who has gone and wed a slave."

H. He said to her, "Who is your father?"

I. She said to him, "I am the daughter of Saddoq, the high priest.

J. He said to her, "Where did you used to live?"

K. She said to him, "In Jerusalem, in the upper market place."

L. He said to her, "What was the mark of the house?"

M. She told him, "Such and so."

N. He said to her, "Did you have a brother or sister?"

O. She said to him, "I had a brother, with a mole on his shoulder. When he would come home from school, I would uncover it and kiss it."

P. He said to her, "If you were to see it, would you recognize it?"

Q. She said to him, "Yes."

R. He bared his shoulder, and they recognized one another, embraced, and kissed, until their souls expired.

S. And the Holy Spirit cried, "For these things I weep."

6. A. There was the case of Miriam [Buber: Martha], daughter of Boethus, that she was betrothed to Joshua b. Gamla, and the king appointed him high priest.

B. He married her.

C. One time she said, "I shall go and see how it reads in the Torah on the Day of Atonement."

D. What did they do for her? They brought out carpets from the door of her house to the door of the house of the sanctuary, so that her feet should not be exposed. Nonetheless, her feet were exposed.

E. When her husband died, sages decreed for her [a settlement of her marriage contract involving] two seahs of wine a day.

F. But it has been taught, "They do not allot wine for a woman by the act of a court." And why not? R. Hiyya b. Abba said, "It is a precaution against wantonness: 'Harlotry, wine, and new wine take away the heart' (Hos. 4:11)."

G. And why then did they allot wine for her? R. Hezeqiah, R. Abbahu in the name of R. Yohanan: "It was for her cooking."

H. And lo, we have learned: But if she was nursing a child, they give her less work to do and give her higher alimony [M. Ket. 5:9F].

I. R. Joshua b. Levi commented [on this passage], "What do they add? Wine, because it makes the milk flow."

J. Said R. Eleazar bar Saddoq, "May I not see consolation, if I did not see that the troops tied her hair on the tails of horses and made her run from Jerusalem to Lud.

K. "In her regard I cited this verse: 'The tender and delicate woman among you, who would not set the sole of her foot on the ground because of delicateness and tenderness' (Dt. 28:56)."

7. A. There was the case of Miriam, daughter of Naqdimon, for whom sages allotted the sum of five hundred gold denars for the purchase of perfumes daily.

B. Nonetheless, she went and cursed them, saying to them, "May you have to make exactly the same allotment to your daughters!"

C. Said R. Aha, "So he replied after her, 'Amen.'"

D. Said R. Eleazar b. R. Saddoq, "May I not see consolation, if I did not see her gathering barley from beneath the hooves of the horses in Acco.

E. "In her regard I cited this verse: 'If you do not know, O you fairest among women, go forth by the footsteps of the flock and feed your kids' (Song 1:8).

F. "Read the consonants for the word 'your kids' as though they spelled 'your bodies' [Cohen, p. 129, n. 4: 'If you know not how to observe the Torah, then the time will come when you will have to go out among the footsteps of the flocks to seek grain to feed your bodies']."

8. A. There is the case of Miriam, daughter of Tanhum, who was taken captive and ransomed in Acco. They brought her a shift, and she went down to immerse in the sea, and the waves came and swept it off, so she got another and went down to immerse in the sea, and the waves came and swept it off.

B. When she saw this, she said, "Let the Collector [God] collect the debt. [The waves exact punishment for my sins.]"

C. Since she had accepted the divine decree upon her self, the Holy One, blessed be he, gestured to the sea and it returned her garments.

9. A. There was the case of Miriam, daughter of Tanhum, who was taken captive with her seven sons with her.

B. The ruler took and imprisoned them within seven rooms.

C. Then he went and brought the eldest and said to him, "Bow down before the idol."

D. He said to him, "God forbid! I will not bow down before the idol."

E. "Why not?"

F. "Because it is written in the Torah, 'I am the Lord your God' (Ex. 20:2)."

G. He forthwith had him taken off and killed.

H. Then he went and brought the next and said to him, "Bow down before the idol."

I. He said to him, "God forbid! I will not bow down before the idol."

J. "Why not?"

K. "Because it is written in the Torah, 'You shall have no other gods before me' (Ex. 20:3)."

L. He forthwith had him taken off and killed.

M. Then he went and brought the next and said to him, "Bow down before the idol."

N. He said to him, "God forbid! I will not bow down before the idol."

O. "Why not?"

P. "Because it is written in the Torah, 'For you shall not bow down to any other god' (Ex. 34:14)."

Q. He forthwith had him taken off and killed.

R. Then he went and brought the next and said to him, "Bow down before the idol."

S. He said to him, "God forbid! I will not bow down before the idol."

T. "Why not?"

U. "Because it is written in the Torah, 'He who sacrifices unto the gods, except for the Lord only, shall be utterly destroyed' (Ex. 22:19)."

V. He forthwith had him taken off and killed.

W. Then he went and brought the next and said to him, "Bow down before the idol."

X. He said to him, "God forbid! I will not bow down before the idol."

Y. "Why not?"

Z. "Because it is written in the Torah, 'Hear, O Israel, the Lord our God, the Lord is one' (Dt. 6:4)."

AA. He forthwith had him taken off and killed.

BB. Then he went and brought the next and said to him, "Bow down before the idol."

CC. He said to him, "God forbid! I will not bow down before the idol."

DD. "Why not?"

EE. "Because it is written in the Torah, 'For the Lord your God is in the midst of you, a God great and awful' (Dt. 7:21).

FF. He forthwith had him taken off and killed.

GG. Then he went and brought the youngest and said to him, "My child, bow down before the idol."

HH. He said to him, "God forbid! I will not bow down before the idol."

II. "Why not?"

JJ. "Because it is written in the Torah, 'Know this day and lay it to your heart that the Lord, he is God in heaven above and on earth beneath, there is none else' (Dt. 4:39).

KK. "Furthermore, we have taken an oath to our God that we will not exchange him for any other: 'You have sworn the Lord this day to be your God' (Dt. 26:17). And as we swore to him, so he swore to us not to exchange us for another people: 'And the Lord has sworn you this day to be his own treasure' (Dt. 26:18)."

LL. He said to him, "[Following Cohen's text, p. 131:] Your brothers have had their fill of years and life and have had happiness, but you are young and have not. Bow down before the idol, and I will show you favor."

MM. He said to him, "It is written in our Torah, 'The Lord shall reign for ever and ever' (Ex. 15:18), 'The Lord is king for ever, the nations have perished out of his land' (Ps. 10:16).

NN. "You are nothing, and his enemies are nothing. A human being lives today and is gone tomorrow, rich today and poor tomorrow, but the Holy One, blessed be he, lives and endures for all eternity."

OO. He said to him, "I will toss my ring to the earth in front of the idol. You just pick it up. Then people will know that you have obeyed Caesar."

PP. He said to him, "Woe to you, Caesar, if you fear mortals, who are no different from you, shall I not fear the King of kings, the Holy One, blessed be he, the God of the universe?"

QQ. He said to him, "And is there a divinity in the world?"

RR. He said to him, "Woe to you, Caesar, and have you seen a world without rules?"

SS. He said to him, "And does your God have a mouth?"

TT. He said to him, "And concerning your idol it is written, 'They have a mouth but cannot speak' (Ps. 115:5). But in connection with our God: 'By the word of the Lord the heavens were made' (Ps. 33:6)."

UU. He said to him, "And does your God have eyes?"

VV. He said to him, "In regard to your idol it is written, 'They have eyes but do not see' (Ps. 115:5) but in connection with our God it is written, 'The eyes of the Lord that run to and fro through the whole earth' (Zech. 4:10)."

WW. He said to him, "And does your God have ears?"

XX. He said to him, "In regard to your idol it is written, 'They have ears but they do not hear' (Ps. 115:6), but in connection with our God it is written, 'And the Lord listened and heard' (Mal. 3:16).'"

YY. He said to him, "And does your God have a nose?"

ZZ. He said to him, "In regard to your idol it is written, 'They have noses but do not smell' (Ps. 115:6), but in connection with our God it is written, 'And the Lord smelled the sweet odor' (Gen. 8:21)."

AAA. He said to him, "And does your God have hands?"

BBB. He said to him, "In regard to your idol it is written, 'They have hands but they do not handle' (Ps. 115:7), but in connection with our God it is written, 'Yes, my hand has laid the foundation of the earth' (Is. 48:13)."

CCC. He said to him, "And does your God have feet?"

DDD. He said to him, "In regard to your idol it is written, 'They have feet but they do not walk' (Ps. 115:7), but in connection with our God it is written, 'And his feet shall stand in that day on the Mount of Olives' (Zech. 14:4)."

EEE. He said to him, "And does your God have a throat?"

FFF. He said to him, "In regard to your idol it is written, 'Neither do they speak with their throat' (Ps. 115:7), but in connection with our God it is written, 'And sound goes out of his mouth' (Job 37:2).

GGG. He said to him, "If he has all of these traits, how come he does not save you from my power as he saved Hananiah, Mishael, and Azariah from the power of Nebuchadnezzar?"

HHH. He said to him, "Hananiah, Mishael, and Azariah were meritorious, and they fell into the hands of a meritorious king, while we are guilty and have fallen into the hands of a guilt-ridden and cruel king.

III. [Following Cohen, p. 132,] "And as for ourselves, our lives are forfeit to heaven. If you do not kill us, the Holy One, blessed be he, has many bears, wolves, snakes, leopards, and scorpions to kill us.

JJJ. "But the Holy One, blessed be he, has given us over into your hand only so as to exact from you vengeance for our blood in the future."

KKK. He immediately gave the order to put him to death.

LLL. His mother said to him, "By your life, Caesar, give me my son, so I may hug and kiss him."

MMM. They gave her her son, and she took out her breasts and gave him milk.

NNN. She said to him, "By your life, Caesar, kill me first, then him."

OOO. He said to her, "I cannot do that, for it is written in your Torah, 'And whether it be cow or ewe, you shall not kill it and its young in one day' (Lev. 22:28)."

PPP. "You wicked man! Now have you kept all of the commandments of the Torah except for this one alone?"

QQQ. He immediately gave the order to put him to death.

RRR. His mother threw herself upon her child and hugged and kissed him, saying to him, "My son, go tell Abraham, our father, 'My mother says to you, "Do not take pride, claiming, I built an altar and offered up my son, Isaac."

SSS. "'Now see, my mother built seven altars and offered up seven sons in one day.

TTT. "'And yours was only a test, but I really had to do it.'"

UUU. While she was hugging him, the king gave the order, and they killed him in her arms.

VVV. When he was put to death, sages calculated the matter of the child's age and found that he was two years, six months, and six and a half hours old [Cohen's reading over Buber's].

WWW. At that moment all the nations of the world cried out and said, "What kind of God do these people have, who does such things to them! 'No, but for your sake, we are killed all day long' (Ps. 44:23)."

XXX. They say that after some days the woman went mad and threw herself from the roof and died: "She who has borne seven languished" (Jer. 15:9).

YYY. An echo came forth: "A joyful mother of children" (Ps. 113:9).

ZZZ. And the Holy Spirit cried, "For these things I weep."

10. A. They said concerning Doeg, son of Joseph, that he died and left a young son to his mother, who would measure him by handbreadths and give his weight in gold to Heaven year by year.

B. When the earthworks besieged Jerusalem, she slaughtered him by her own hand and ate him.

C. And in her regard Jeremiah laments, saying, "See, Lord, and consider to whom you have done this? Shall women eat their fruit, the children that are dandled in the hands?" (Lam. 2:20).

D. And the Holy Spirit answered, "Shall the priest and prophet be slain in the sanctuary of the Lord?" (Zech. 2:20),

E. with reference to Zechariah son of Jehoiada.

11. A. Another interpretation of the phrase, "For these things I weep":

B. R. Judah and R. Nehemiah:

C. R. Judah says, "[The weeping is] for the departure of all sound senses and the departure of the Presence of God.

D. "Zedekiah was standing and seeing his sons slaughtered before him, and seeing others put out his eyes, and would he not have the sense to beat his head against the wall until he died?

E. "But he allowed his sons to be slain in his presence [without committing suicide]: 'The heart of the king shall fall and the heart of the princes' (Jer. 4:9)."

F. R. Nehemiah says, "It is for the departure of the priesthood and kingship:

G. "'These are the two anointed ones, who stand by the Lord of the whole earth' (Zech. 4:14), referring to Aaron and David.

H. "Aaron lays claim in behalf of his priesthood, David for his monarchy."

I. R. Joshua b. Levi said, "It is for the departure of the Torah: 'These ['For these things I weep'] are the statutes and the ordinances' (Dt. 12:1)."

J. R. Samuel b. Nahmani said, "It was for idolatry: 'This ['For these things I weep'] is your God, O Israel' (Ex. 32:4)."

K. Zabdi b. Levi said, "It was for the departure of the sacrifices: 'These ['For these things I weep'] you shall offer to the Lord in your appointed seasons' (Num. 29:39)."

L. Rabbis say, "It was for the departure of the Levitical watches."

M. What good did those watches do?

N. On Monday they fasted for the safety of those who were on journeys by sea, on Tuesday, for those on journeys by land, on Wednesday, for children not to be sick with croup and die, on Thursday for pregnant women not to miscarry and nursing mothers' children not to die.

O. But can one fast for two purposes at the same time? But it is written, "So we fasted and asked our God for this" (Ezra 8:23) [this one thing], and so too: "That they might ask mercy from the God of heaven concerning this secret" (Dan. 2:18) — one, not two secrets!

P. R. Hiyya b. Abba said, "One may fast at one and the same time both concerning the withholding of rain and also

concerning the exile, but on Friday or the Sabbath one
may not fast, because of the honor owing to the Sabbath."

These stories coming to an end, we proceed to read our verse
in the manner of exegetes, explaining the sense of the verses in an
expository manner rather than through narrative:

12. A. "my eyes flow with tears":
    B. Said R. Levi, "The matter may be compared to the case
       of a physician who had one bad eye [which was watery].
       He said, 'My one eye weeps for my other eye.'
    C. "So the Israelites are called 'the eye of the Holy One,
       blessed be he': 'For the Lord's is the eye of man and all
       the tribes of Israel' (Zech. 9:1).
    D. "It is as though the Holy One, blessed be he, said, 'My
       one eye weeps for my other eye.'"

Our sages, of course, identify "comforter," "savior," "Messiah,"
and the like, and any reference to the one will provoke thought
about all the others. They never conceived that there would be only
one Messiah; "Messiah" formed a category, as did "Savior," and they
could identify Mordecai with David as much as with "the Royal
Messiah." There was no conception that there was, or could be, only
one, unique Messiah at the end of time.

13. A. "for a comforter is far from me, one to revive my cour-
       age":
    B. What is the name of the royal messiah?
    C. R. Abba bar Kahana said, "The Lord is his name: 'And
       this is the name with which he shall be called: "The Lord
       is our righteousness"'' (Jer. 23:66)."
    D. For R. Levi said, "Fortunate is the city that bears the name
       of its king, that the king of which bears the name of
       its God.
    E. "'Fortunate is the city that bears the name of its king:
       "And the name of the city from that day shall be the Lord
       is there" (Ez. 48:35).

F. " 'that the king of which bears the name of its God: And this is the name with which he shall be called: "The Lord is our righteousness" ' (Jer. 23:66)."

G. R. Joshua said, "His name is 'shoot': 'Behold, a man whose name is Shoot, and who shall shoot up out of his place and build the Temple of the Lord' (Zech. 6:12)."

H. R. Yudan in the name of R. Aibu: "His name is Comforter: 'for a comforter is far from me, one to revive my courage.' "

I. R. Hanina said, "They do not in fact differ. The numerical value of the letters of the several names is the same, 'Comforter' having the same numerical value as 'Shoot.' "

We move to a narrative to amplify the matter under discussion.

14. A. The following case sustains the position of R. Yudan in the name of R. Aibu:

B. There was a man who was ploughing, and one of his oxen lowed.

C. An Arab came by and said to him, "What are you?"

D. He said to him, "I am a Jew."

E. He said to him, "Untie your ox and your plough."

F. He said to him, "Why?"

G. He said to him, "Because the house of the sanctuary of the Jews has been destroyed."

H. He said to him, "How do you know?"

I. He said to him, "I know from the lowing of your ox."

J. While he was engaged with him, the ox lowed again.

K. He said to him, "Harness your ox and tie on your plough, for the redeemer of the Jews has been born."

L. He said to him, "What is his name?"

M. He said to him, "His name is Menahem [Redeemer]."

N. "And as to his father, what is his name?"

O. He said to him, "Hezekiah."

P. He said to him, "And where do they live?"

Q. He said to him, "In Birat Arba in Bethlehem in Judah."

R. That man went and sold his oxen and sold his plough and bought felt clothing for children. He went into one city and left another, went into one country and left another, until he got there. All the villagers came to buy from him. But the woman who was the mother of that infant did not buy from him. He said to her, "Why didn't you buy children's felt clothing from me?"

S. She said to him, "Because [Cohen, p. 137:] a hard fate is in store for my child."

T. He said to her, "Why?"

U. She said to him, "Because at his coming the house of the sanctuary was destroyed."

V. He said to her, "We trust in the Master of the world that just as at his coming it was destroyed, so at his coming it will be rebuilt."

W. He said to her, "Now you take for yourself some of these children's felt garments."

X. She said to him, "I haven't got any money."

Y. He said to her, "What difference does it make to you! Take them now, and after a few days I'll come and collect."

Z. She took the clothes and went away. After a few days that man said, "I'm going to go and see how that infant is doing."

AA. He came to her and said to her, "As to that child, how is he doing?"

BB. She said to him, "Didn't I tell you that [Cohen, p. 137] a hard fate is in store for him? Misfortune has dogged him.

CC. "From the moment [you left], strong winds have come and a whirlwind and swept him off and have gone on."

DD. He said to her, "Did I not say to you that just as at his coming it was destroyed, so at his coming it will be rebuilt?"

15. A. Said R. Abun, "Why should I have to derive from an Arab [support for the position of R. Aibu, ["His name is Comforter: 'for a comforter is far from me, one to revive my courage' "],

B. "for is there not an explicit verse of scripture that says, 'And Lebanon shall fall by a mighty one' (Is. 10:34), followed by 'And there shall come forth a shoot out of the stock of Jesse and a twig shall grow forth out of his roots' (Is. 11:1) [and that shows that the day on which the Temple is destroyed, the Messiah will be born (Cohen, p. 137, n. 5)]."

16. A. The school of R. Shila says, "Shila is the name of the messiah: 'Until Shiloh comes' (Gen. 49:10),

B. "and the word is spelled with the consonants used in the name of Shila."

17. A. The school of R. Hanina says, "His name is Haninah: 'I will not give you Haninah' (Jer. 16:13)."

18. A. The school of R. Yannai says, "His name is Yinnon: 'Before the sun was, his name is Yinnon' (Ps. 72:17) [following Cohen, p. 138]."

19. A. R. Biba of Sergunieh says, "His name is Nehirah: 'And the light [nehorah] dwells with him' (Dan. 2:22), and the word for light is spelled nehirah."

20. A. R. Judah b. R. Simon said in the name of R. Samuel bar Isaac, "That royal messiah, whether he is of the living, is named David, and whether he is among the dead, is named David."

B. Said R. Tanhuma, "I shall state a verse of scripture that shows that fact: 'Great salvation he gives to his king and shows mercy to his messiah' (Ps. 18:51), going on to say not 'and to David' but 'to David and his descendants forever more.'"

21. A. "my children are desolate, for the enemy has prevailed":

B. R. Aibu said, "It is like the tuber of a cabbage.

C. "As the cabbage increases in size, the tuber shrinks."

D. R. Judah b. R. Simon said, "It is like a sow that shrinks as the litter grows."

Because of the heavy interpolations, the treatment of our base verse is enormous; "for these things I weep" invites a long sequence of martyrologies, Nos. 1, 2, 3 (which serves Ez. 5:10), 4, 5; these are enriched with materials on how the spoiled suffered in particular, Nos. 6, 7, 8, and 10, and these items serve Deuteronomy 28:56 and related verses; then another, and principal, martyrology, Hannah and her seven sons, parachuted down with no clear reason other than a general thematic affinity, Nos. 8–9. No. 11 reverts back to the base verse, as though we had been given anything remotely suggesting an amplification of a disciplined character, and No. 12 moves us on to the next clause. Here we do find something enriching, which is the recurrent interest in showing how God suffers with Israel and for Israel. No. 13 then proceeds to the next theme — one can hardly call it a sustained amplification of anything to do with the cited verse. This yields a sizable interpolation of Messiah materials, none of them pretending to have been framed for the purposes of our document. The sequence runs from No. 13 to the end. Only No. 21 reverts to our base verse with what we can call a simple exegesis.

8

Parashah II
Lamentations 2:2

The Lord has destroyed without mercy
all the habitations of Jacob;
in his wrath he has broken down the strongholds
of the daughter of Judah;
he has brought down to the ground in dishonor
the kingdom and its rulers.

We take up an intersecting verse for the reading of the base verse cited above. Why has God not had pity on Jacob? Israel atones for sins committed long ago, for the sin of the golden calf, with atonement persisting even to the time of the destruction. So we begin with the question, how long will it be before the golden calf is atoned for?

LVIII.i.

    1. A. ["The Lord has destroyed without mercy all the habitations of Jacob; in his wrath he has broken down the

strongholds of the daughter of Judah; he has brought down to the ground in dishonor the kingdom and its rulers":]

B. "Then he called loudly in my hearing, saying, 'Approach, you men in charge of the city, each bearing his weapons of destruction.' [And six men entered by way of the upper gate that faces north, each with his club in his hand; and among them was another, clothed in linen, with a writing case at his waist. They came forward and stopped at the bronze altar. Now the Presence of the God of Israel had moved from the cherub on which it had rested to the platform of the house. He called to the man clothed in linen with the writing case at his waist; and the Lord said to him, 'Pass through the city, through Jerusalem, and put a mark on the foreheads of the men who moan and groan because of all the abominations that are committed in it.' To the others he said in my hearing, 'Follow him through the city and strike; show no pity or compassion. Kill off graybeard, youth and maiden, women and children; but do not touch any person who bears the mark. Begin here at my sanctuary.' So they began with the elders who were in front of the house. And he said to them, 'Defile the House and fill the courts with the slain. Then go forth.' So they went forth and began to kill in the city. When they were out killing, and I remained alone, I flung myself on my face and cried out, 'Ah, Lord God, are you going to annihilate all that is left of Israel, pouring our your fury upon Jerusalem?' He answered me, 'The iniquity of the Houses of Judah and Israel is very, very great, the land is full of crime, and the city is full of corruption. For they say, "The Lord has forsaken the land, and the Lord does not see"']" (Ez. 9:1–8):

C. Until what time did the [penalty because of] the sin of the golden calf last?

D. Said R. Berekhiah, and some say, R. Nehemiah b. Eleazar, "To the time of the calves made by Jeroboam, son of Nebat: 'When I would heal Israel, then is the iniquity

of Ephraim uncovered and the wickedness of Samaria'
(Hos. 7:1).

E. "Said the Holy One, blessed be he, 'I came to heal Israel
from the sin that it committed through the calf, but now
'the iniquity of Ephraim is uncovered.'"

F. R. Ishmael b. Nahmani in the name of R. Yohanan said,
"It was up to the destruction of the house of the sanctuary: 'Cause the visitations of the city to draw near, every
man with his destroying weapon in his hand' (Ez. 9:1).
'Nevertheless in the day when I visit, I will visit their sin
upon them' (Ex. 32:34)."

2. A. "And six men entered by way of the upper gate that
faces north, each with his club in his hand; and among
them was another, clothed in linen, with a writing case at
his waist. They came forward and stopped at the bronze
altar":

B. [While they are six,] are not the decrees five? "Follow
him through the city and strike; show no pity or compassion. Kill off graybeard, youth and maiden, women and
children."

C. Said R. Yohanan, "He said this to the angel who is
the most harsh, Gabriel: 'and among them was another,
clothed in linen, with a writing case at his waist.'

D. "He did three jobs: scribe, executioner, and high priest.

E. "Scribe: 'with a writing case at his waist.'

F. "Executioner: 'He has utterly destroyed them, he has
delivered them to the slaughter' (Is. 34:2).

G. "High priest: 'and among them was another, clothed in
linen.'"

3. A. "each with his club in his hand":

B. Weapons for fighting, destruction, sending into exile.

C. For fighting: "each with his club in his hand."

D. For destruction: "When he makes all the stones of the
altar as chalkstones that are beaten in pieces" (Is. 27:9).

E. For sending into exile: "You are my maul and weapons of
war" (Jer. 51:20).

4. A. "They came forward and stopped at the bronze altar":

B. R. Judah b. R. Simon says, "To the end of the area in which they were permitted" [Cohen, p. 154: "To the end of their permitted area" and see his n. 2].

C. Rabbis say, "He means to call to mind the sins of Ahaz: 'And king Ahaz commanded Uriah the priest, saying... but the bronze altar shall be for me to look to' (2 Kgs. 16:15)."

D. What is the sense of "for me to look to"?

E. R. Phineas said, "He made it unfit and put blemishes on the animals: 'The priest shall not look to the yellow hair, he is unclean' (Lev. 13:36)."

5. A. "and the Lord said to him, Pass through the city, through Jerusalem":

B. The word for "to him" is written as though it were to be pronounced, "to his strong one."

C. Said R. Simeon b. Laqish, "To the angel who was the harshest of them all he spoke, that is, Gabriel."

6. A. "and put a mark":

B. It is to be a tav [the last letter of the Hebrew alphabet].

C. R. Nahman said, "This refers to people who kept the Torah from alef [the first letter of the Hebrew alphabet] to tav."

D. Rabbis say, "[Cohen, p. 154:] It was the word of condemnation."

E. Rab said, "Since he used the tav in all cases, it could represent 'be dismayed' or 'live' [since both words begin with that same letter]."

F. R. Hanina b. Isaac said, "It stands for 'ended is the merit of the ancestors' [since the word for merit begins with the same letter]."

7. A. [Following Cohen, p. 155:] [supply "who moan and groan because of all the abominations that are committed in it":]

B. R. Hoshaiah sent word to R. Simon, "Because you are part of the administration of the exilarch, why don't you rebuke them for their sins?"

C. He said to him, "Would that we were among those of whom it is written, 'who moan and groan because of all the abominations that are committed in it.'"

D. He said to him, "Will the punishment not begin with them? 'To the others he said in my hearing, Follow him through the city and strike; show no pity or compassion.'"

8. A. [Supply: "To the others he said in my hearing":]

B. Said R. Eleazar, "The Holy One, blessed be he, never joins his name with what is wicked but only with what is good.

C. "What is written here is not, 'God said in my hearing,' but 'To the others he said in my hearing.'"

9. A. [Supply: "Follow him through the city and strike; show no pity or compassion. Kill off graybeard, youth and maiden, women and children; but do not touch any person who bears the mark. Begin here at my sanctuary":]

B. [If it says to mark the ones who are not to be smitten, then why begin at the sanctuary, where righteous people are expected to take refuge?] How so?

C. At that moment the prosecutor leapt before the Holy One, blessed be he, and said to him, "Lord of the world? [From Buber's text: How can you show pity on them?] Which of them had his head split open on your account? Which of them gave his life for your name?"

D. He said to him, "Against none of them applies a document [that decrees destruction]."

E. R. Aibu said, "The Holy One, blessed be he, said to him, 'Let the Temple be wiped out, but let no hand touch the righteous.'"

F. R. Judah b. R. Simon said, "[He said,] 'Both the house of the sanctuary and the people are subject to a document [that decrees destruction].'"

10. A. [Supply: "'Begin here at my sanctuary.' So they began with the elders who were in front of the house. And he said to them, 'Defile the house and fill the courts with the slain. Then go forth.' So they went forth and began to kill in the city. When they were out killing, and I remained alone, I flung myself on my face and cried out, 'Ah, Lord

God, are you going to annihilate all that is left of Israel, pouring our your fury upon Jerusalem?' He answered me, 'The iniquity of the houses of Judah and Israel is very, very great, the land is full of crime, and the city is full of corruption. For they say, The Lord has forsaken the land, and the Lord does not see' ":] R. Tanhuma b. Abba in the name of R. Abba: "The Holy One, blessed be he, never made a promise and then went back on it, but in this case it did happen:

B. " 'Begin here at my sanctuary': read the word not as though it spelled, 'at my sanctuary' but 'with my sanctified ones.' [That is, 'begin with my saints.']

C. "And what follows? 'So they began with the elders who were in front of the house. And he said to them, Defile the house and fill the courts with the slain. Then go forth. So they went forth and began to kill in the city.' "

11. A. "When they were out killing, and I remained alone, I flung myself on my face and cried out, Ah, Lord God, are you going to annihilate all that is left of Israel":

B. "all that is left" refers to the righteous.

12. A. At that moment [Jeremiah] came and said, "The Lord has destroyed without mercy all the habitations of Jacob."

The intersecting verse expands on the theme of the Lord's destroying without mercy, and the composition, though somewhat extended, is disciplined and systematic. The elements of the intersecting verse are carefully expounded, and then we revert to the base verse in a precise and appropriate way. No. 1 does not begin with a citation of the base verse, but (as the text translated by Cohen has it) simply the intersecting verse. I have given the whole of it to underline the systematic character of what follows. While it appears that in No. 1 the intersecting verse is subordinated and serves only as a proof text, in fact the entire unit fits extremely well, as 1.F shows. The rest then remains closely linked, clause by clause, to Ezekiel's vision of the destruction. Nos. 9–11 then draw us back to our base verse and its stress that all was done without a trace of divine mercy. I do not know a better example of the power of the form at hand to expose through the intersecting verse the fundamental sense of the base verse, and to do so with great effect. We now proceed to the more familiar second mode of exposition, the one in which the base verse is illustrated and extended, but not expanded through the insertion of an intersecting verse.

LVIII:ii.

1. A. "The Lord has destroyed without mercy all the habitations of Jacob":

   B. R. Phineas in the name of R. Hoshaiah says, "There were four hundred eighty synagogues in Jerusalem, corresponding to the numerical value of the letters in the world 'full,' in the verse, 'She that was full of justice' (Is. 1:21).

   C. "In each synagogue was a school and house of learning, a school for scripture, a house of learning for the Mishnah [and these were the habitations of Jacob]."

2. A. Another interpretation of the verse, "The Lord has destroyed without mercy all the habitations of Jacob":

   B. All of [Cohen, p. 157:] the celebrities of the house of Jacob:

   C. R. Ishmael, Rabban Gamaliel, R. Yeshebab, R. Judah b. Baba, R. Huspit the Interpreter, R. Haninah b. Teradion, R. Aqiba, Ben Azzai, and R. Tarfon.

   D. Some drop R. Tarfon and add R. Eleazar b. Harsom.

What follows is another set of stories about the destruction of Israel by Vespasian and Titus in the war of 67–73, climaxed by the destruction of the Temple in 70. None of this carries forward the foregoing reading of verses. The purpose of our sages in compiling a reading of Lamentations was not only to set Lamentations into the framework of their own experience, that is, reading the book in terms of the destruction of the second Temple and also the war of Bar Kokhba against Hadrian in 132–35. (We note the introduction of the Messiah theme once more, now with the false Messiah, Bar Kokhba.) But also it was to provide an occasion to rehearse that destruction and its heroic moments, not in the framework of a commentary, but in the setting of a sequence of moving stories.

3. A. Rabbi [Judah the Patriarch] would interpret in twenty-four aspects the verse, "The Lord has destroyed without mercy all the habitations of Jacob."

C. R. Yohanan would interpret the verse in sixty ways.

D. Is the number of R. Yohanan then not greater than that of Rabbi?

E. Rabbi, who lived nearer to the time of the destruction of the sanctuary, would remember the anguish and weep as he interpreted, and he would have to be comforted and so would break off.

4. A. Rabbi would interpret the verse, "There shall come forth a star out of Jacob" (Num. 24:17) in this way: "Do not read the letters of the word for 'star' as 'star' but as 'deceit.'"

5. A. When R. Aqiba saw Bar Koziba, he said, "This is the royal messiah."

B. R. Yohanan b. Torta said to him, "Aqiba, grass will grow from your cheeks and he will still not have come."

6. A. R. Yohanan interpreted the verse, "The voice is the voice of Jacob" (Gen. 27:22) in this way: "The voice is the voice of Caesar Hadrian, who killed eighty thousand myriads of people at Betar."

7. A. Eighty thousand trumpeters besieged Betar. There Bar Koziba was encamped, with two hundred thousand men with amputated fingers.

B. Sages sent word to him, saying, "How long are you going to produce blemished men in Israel?"

C. He said to them, "And what shall I do to examine them [to see whether or not they are brave]?"

D. They said to him, "Whoever cannot uproot a cedar of Lebanon do not enroll in your army."

E. He had two hundred thousand men of each sort [half with amputated fingers, half proved by uprooting a cedar].

8. A. When they went out to battle, he would say, "Lord of all ages, don't help us and don't hinder us!"

B. That is in line with this verse: "Have you not, O God, cast us off? And do not go forth, O God, with our hosts" (Ps. 60:12).

9. A. What did Bar Koziba do?

B. He could catch a missile from the enemy's catapult on one of his knees and throw it back, killing many of the enemy.

C. That is why R. Aqiba said what he said [about Bar Koziba's being the royal messiah].

10. A. For three and a half years Hadrian besieged Betar.

B. R. Eleazar the Modiite was sitting in sackcloth and ashes, praying, and saying, "Lord of all the ages, do not sit in judgment today, do not sit in judgment today."

C. Since [Hadrian] could not conquer the place, he considered going home.

D. There was with him a Samaritan, who said to him, "My lord, as long as that old cock wallows in ashes, you will not conquer the city.

E. "But be patient, and I shall do something so you can conquer it today."

F. He went into the gate of the city and found R. Eleazar standing in prayer.

G. He pretended to whisper something into his ear, but the other paid no attention to him.

H. People went and told Bar Koziba, "Your friend wants to betray the city."

I. He sent and summoned the Samaritan and said to him, "What did you say to him?"

J. He said to him, "If I say, Caesar will kill me, and if not, you will kill me. Best that I kill myself and not betray state secrets."

K. Nonetheless, Bar Koziba reached the conclusion that he wanted to betray the city.

L. When R. Eleazar had finished his prayer, he sent and summoned him, saying to him, "What did this one say to you?"

M. He said to him, "I never saw that man."

N. He kicked him and killed him.

O. At that moment an echo proclaimed: "Woe to the worthless shepherd who leaves the flock, the sword shall be upon his arm and upon his right eye" (Zech. 11:17).

P. Said the Holy One, blessed be he, "You have broken the right army of Israel and blinded their right eye. Therefore your arm will wither and your eye grow dark."

Q. Forthwith Betar was conquered and Ben Koziba was killed.

R. They went, carrying his head to Hadrian. He said, "Who killed this one?"

S. They said, "One of the Goths killed him," but he did not believe them.

T. He said to them, "Go and bring me his body."

U. They went to bring his body and found a snake around the neck.

V. He said, "If the God of this one had not killed him, who could have vanquished him?"

W. That illustrates the following verse of scripture: "If their Rock had not given them over..." (Dt. 32:30).

11. A. [Following the order in Cohen, rather than in Buber, who assigns the following to a place after No. 14.F.] They killed the inhabitants of Betar until their horses waded in blood up to their nostrils, and blood rolled along in stones the size of forty-seahs [a huge measure] and flowed into the sea for a distance of four miles.

B. And should you suppose that Betar was near the sea, it was four miles away.

12. A. Hadrian owned a vineyard eighteen miles square, from Tiberias to Sepphoris.

B. They surrounded it with a fence made of the bones of those killed at Betar.

13. A. Nor was it permitted that they might be buried until a certain king came and ordered it.

B. R. Huna said, "On the day on which those killed at Betar were handed over for burial, they invoked the benediction, '... who are kind and deals kindly' [in the Grace after meals]."

C. "'. . . who are kind': because the bodies had not putrefied.

D. "'. . . and who deals kindly': because they were handed over for burial."

14. A. For fifty-two years Betar held out after the destruction of the house of the sanctuary.

B. And why was it destroyed?

C. Because they lit lamps on the occasion of the destruction of the house of the sanctuary.

15. A. [The following story explains why the inhabitants of Betar hated Jerusalem.] They say that there was a place in which the councillors of Jerusalem would go into session, in the center of the city.

B. Someone from Betar would go up for prayer, and they would say, "Do you want to become a councillor?"

C. He said, "No."

D. Someone would say to him, "Would you like to become a city magistrate?"

E. He said, "No."

F. Some would say to him, "I heard you have an estate for sale. Will you sell it to me?"

G. He would say, "I never thought of it."

H. The Jerusalemites would write out and send a deed of possession to the steward of the man from Betar, bearing the message, "If so-and-so [the owner] comes, do not let him enter the property, for he has sold it to me."

I. The man would exclaim, "Would that my leg had been broken, so that I could not have gone up to that corner."

J. That illustrates the verse of scripture: "Our steps were checked, [we could not walk in our squares. Our doom is near, our days are done, alas, our doom has come]" (Lam. 4:18).

16. A. ["Our steps were checked, we could not walk in our squares. Our doom is near, our days are done, alas, our doom has come" (Lam. 4:18):]

B. "Our steps were checked":

C. [Since the letters in the word for "checked" may be read as "hunt" or as "desolate,"] "May the road to Jerusalem become desolate, so that none "could walk in our squares."

D. "Our doom is near":

E. "May the end of this Temple be near."

F. "our days are done":

G. "May the days of this Temple be done."

H. But with them things did not go well: "He who is glad at calamity shall not go unpunished" (Prov. 17:5).

17. A. R. Yohanan said, "They found the brains of three hundred children dashed upon one rock,

B. "and three hundred baskets of tefillin-boxes, each basket holding three seahs, so that there were nine hundred seahs."

18. A. Rabban Simeon b. Gamaliel said, "There were five hundred schools in Betar, and in the smallest of them there were three hundred children.

B. "The children would say, 'When the enemy comes against us, with these styluses we shall go out to do battle with them and stab them.'

C. "But when sin brought it about that the enemy came against them, they wrapped up each child in his book and burned him, and I alone survived.

D. "In his own regard he recited this verse: 'My eye affected my soul, because of all the daughters of my city' (Lam. 3:51)."

19. A. There were two brothers in Kefar Haruba, and no Roman could pass by there, for they killed him.

B. They decided, "The whole point of the thing is that we must take the crown and put it on our head and make ourselves kings."

C. They heard that the Romans were coming to fight them.

D. They went out to do battle, and an old man met them and said, "May the Creator be your help against them."

E. They said, "Let him not help us nor hinder us!"

F. Because of their sins, they went forth and were killed.

G. They went, carrying his head to Hadrian. He said, "Who killed this one?"

H. They said, "One of the Goths killed him," but he did not believe them.

I. He said to them, "Go and bring me his body."

J. They went to bring his body and found a snake around the neck.

L. He said, "If the God of this one had not killed him, who could have vanquished him?"

M. That illustrates the following verse of scripture: "If their Rock had not given them over..." (Dt. 32:30).

20. A. There were two cedars on the Mount of Olives.

B. Under one of them were four shops of those who sold [birds required for rites of] purification.

C. Under the second they produced forty seahs of pigeons month by month.

D. [Cohen, p. 162:] Simeon would distribute three hundred barrels [of thin cakes among the poor every Friday]. [Buber places this item after No. 21.]

E. Why then were such places wiped out?

F. Should you say that it was because of the hookers, is it not the case that there was only one such girl there, and they threw her out?

G. Said R. Hun, "It is because on the Sabbath they would play a ball game."

21. A. There were ten thousand townships in the royal mountain-range.

B. R. Eleazar b. Harsom had a thousand of them, and, as their counterpart, a thousand ships on the sea.

22. A. [Cohen, p. 162:] The taxes of three of these towns, Kabul, Shihin, and Magdala, had to be carried to Jerusalem in a wagon....

D. Why was Kabul destroyed?

E. Because of dissension.

F. Shihin?

G. Because of witchcraft.

H. Magdala?

I. Because of fornication.

23. A. There were three towns in the south, each with a population twice that of those who had gone forth from Egypt: Kefar Bish, Kefar Shihlayim, and Kefar Dikrin.

   B. Why is it called Kefar Bish? [It was called "Bad Town"] because they were bad to visitors.

   C. Why was it called Kefar Shihlayim? [It was called "Watercressville"] because in that town every woman had a lot of children, as abundant as watercress.

   D. Why was it called Kefar Dikrin? [It was called "Boys Town"] because in that town the women produced a lot of sons.

   E. Any one of them who wanted to have a daughter would go out of town and there produce the daughter, and any woman from elsewhere who wanted a son would go there and produce the son.

   F. And if [today] you wanted to put sixty myriads of reeds there, the place could not hold them.

   G. Said R. Yohanan, "The land of Israel shrank."

24. A. Said R. Huna, "There were three hundred shops for selling [birds required for rites of] purification in Madgala of the Dyers,

   B. "and three hundred shops of curtain-weavers in Kefar Nimrah."

25. A. Said R. Jeremiah in the name of R. Hiyya b. Abba, "There were eighty brothers of the priestly caste who married eighty counterparts, sisters of the priestly caste, in a single night in the town of Gofnit.

   B. "That is besides the brothers without sisters, sisters without brothers, Levites, and ordinary Israelites."

26. A. Said R. Yohanan, "Eighty thousand younger priests were killed on account of the blood of Zechariah."

   B. R. Yudan asked R. Aha, "Where did the Israelites kill Zechariah? Was it in the courtyard of women or in the courtyard of the Israelites?"

   C. He said to him, "It was neither in the women's courtyard nor in the Israelites' courtyard, but in the priests' courtyard. But they did not dispose of his blood like the blood of a hin or a ram: 'He shall pour out the blood thereof and cover it with dust' (Lev. 17:13).

D. "But here: 'For the blood she shed is still in her; she set it upon a bare rock; she did not pour it out on the ground to cover it with earth' (Ez. 24:7).

E. "'She set her blood upon the bare rock, so that it was not covered, so that it may stir up my fury to take vengeance' (Ez. 24:8)."

F. "And why so? 'That it might cause fury to come up, that vengeance might be taken, I have set her blood upon the bare rock, that it should not be covered' (Ez. 24:8)."

27. A. Seven transgressions did the Israelites commit on that day: they murdered [1] a priest, [2] prophet, [3] judge, [4] they spilled innocent blood, [5] they blasphemed the divine name, [6] they imparted uncleanness to the court-yard, and it was, furthermore, [7] a Day of Atonement that coincided with the Sabbath.

B. When Nebuzaradan came in, the blood began to drip. He said to them, "What sort of blood is this dripping blood?"

C. They said to him, "It is the blood of oxen, rams, and sheep that we offered on the altar."

D. He forthwith sent and brought oxen, rams, and sheep and slaughtered them in his presence, but the blood continued to drip. [Cohen, p. 164: the blood did not behave similarly]. He had all kinds of animals brought, but the blood did not behave similarly.

E. He said to them, "If you tell the truth, well and good, but if not, I shall comb your flesh with iron combs."

F. They said to him, "What shall we tell you? He was a prophet-priest who rebuked us in the name of Heaven: 'Submit, but we did not submit.' We conspired against him and killed him. And lo, years have passed, but his blood has not stopped seething."

G. He said to them, "I shall appease it."

H. He brought before him the great sanhedrin and the lesser

sanhedrin and killed them, [until their blood mingled with that of Zechariah: "Oaths are imposed and broken, they kill and rob, there is nothing but adultery and licence, one deed of blood after another (Hos. 4:2).] He had the young priests brought and killed them by it, but it did not stop.

I. Still the blood seethed. He brought boys and girls and killed them by the blood, but it did not stop seething.

J. He brought youngsters from the school house and killed them over it, but it did not stop seething.

K. Forthwith he took eighty thousand young priests and killed them on his account, until the blood lapped the grave of Zechariah. But the blood did not stop seething.

L. He said, "Zechariah, Zechariah, All the best of them I have destroyed. Do you want me to exterminate them all?"

M. When he said this, the blood forthwith came to rest.

N. Then the evil Nebuzaradan considered repenting, saying, "Now if one soul matters so, that in connection with one who destroys a single Israelite life it is written, 'Whoever sheds blood by man shall his blood be shed' (Gen. 9:6), as to that man who has killed all these souls, how much the more so!"

O. Forthwith the Holy One, blessed be he, was filled with mercy and signaled to the blood, which immediately absorbed itself into the ground.

27. A. Eighty thousand young priests, carrying eighty thousand gold shields, broke through the armies of Nebuchadnezzar and escaped to the Ishmaelites.

B. They said to them, "Give us some water."

C. They said to them, "Eat first, then you drink."

D. What did they do? They produced salty foods. After they had eaten, they produced for them blown-up skin bottles.

E. When one of them put it to his mouth, the air rushed into his belly, and he writhed and died.

F. That is in line with the following: "The burden upon

Arabia. In the thickets in Arabia you shall lodge, O you caravans of Dedanites. To him who is thirsty you bring water! The inhabitants of the land of Tema met the fugitives with his bread" (Is. 21:13).

G. "Who allowed you to lodge in the evening in the forest of Lebanon?"

H. "O you caravans of Dedanites": "Should caravans made up of children of Dedanites act in such a way? Did the father act in this way to your father?

I. "In regard to your father it is written, 'And God opened her eyes, and she saw a well of water, and she went and filled the bottle with water and gave the child something to drink' (Gen. 21:19).

J. "But that is not what you did in response to the saying, 'To him who is thirsty you bring water!'

K. "Did they want to come to you? 'They fled from the swords' (Is. 21:15) — the sword of Nebuchadnezzar.

L. "'From the drawn sword': This was because they did not observe the sabbatical years correctly: 'But the seventh year you shall let it rest and lie fallow' (Ex. 23:11). [The words for 'lie fallow' and 'sword' use the same consonants]."

M. This was because they did not keep the Sabbath in the right way: "In those days I saw in Judah some who were treading winepresses on the Sabbath" (Neh. 13:15).

N. [Continuing L:] "'And from the grief of war' (Is. 21:15): because they did not engage in the struggle in the warfare of the Torah: 'Wherefore it is said in the books of the wars of the Lord' (Num. 21:14)."

28. A. Said R. Yohanan, "Between Gibbethon and Antipatris were sixty myriads of townships. There is no smaller among them than Bet Shemesh: 'And he smote of the men of Beth Shemesh . . . seventy men and fifty thousand men' (1 Sam. 6:19).

B. "But now there is scarcely space there for a hundred reeds."

C. Said R. Yohanan, "Its priestly watch was the smallest of them all, yet it yielded eighty thousand young priests."

29. A. How many battles did Hadrian fight in the land of Israel?
    B. Two Amoras differed on the matter.
    C. One of them said, "Fifty-two."
    D. The other said, "Fifty-four."
30. A. Said R. Yohanan, "Happy is the person who has the merit of seeing the downfall of Palmyra.
    B. "Why so? Because it produced archers for the destruction of the house of the sanctuary."
    C. And how many archers did it produce?
    D. R. Yudan and R. Huna:
    E. R. Yudan said, "Eighty thousand archers it produced for the destruction of the first Temple, and forty thousand for the second.
    F. R. Huna said, Forty thousand for the first and forty thousand for the second."

The base verse refers to destroying without mercy all the habitations of Jacob, and that provokes an essay on the extent of the destruction — what was destroyed, the rich country and population — and the way in which it was destroyed — without mercy. The entire composition, which runs on, is parachuted down; there is scarcely any pretense at exegesis. The complex of Bar Kokhba materials, Nos. 4ff., allows the last catastrophe to be introduced in the setting of the book of Lamentations. An exegesis of Isaiah 21:13 finds its place in No. 27, but this seems to me garbled and out of place; No. 27 should really end at F. Then from that point we have a distinct exercise, an exegesis of Isaiah 21:13–15. But K draws us back to the earlier material. In all, the entire composite draws us far from the text that provides the structure for the whole. But that is hardly surprising, given the intent of the ultimate compilers of the document. But now back to the main structure of exposition: the verse and its meanings.

LVIII:iii.

1. A. "in his wrath he has broken down the strongholds of the daughter of Judah; [he has brought down to the ground in dishonor the kingdom and its rulers]":

B. R. Yudah said, "Every stronghold in Jerusalem was such that it should have taken forty days to conquer it."

C. R. Phineas said, "Fifty days."

D. But sin made it so that "he has brought down to the ground in dishonor the kingdom and its rulers."

2. A. "he has brought down to the ground in dishonor the kingdom and its rulers":

B. "the kingdom": refers to the Israelites: "And you shall be to me a kingdom of priests and a holy people" (Ex. 19:6).

3. A. "and its rulers":

B. This refers to the rulers above.

4. A. You find that when Jeremiah prophesied to the Israelites, saying to them, "Repent before the enemy comes against you," they would say to him, "If the enemy comes, what can they do against us?"

B. He said to them, "I will surround the city with a wall of water":

C. Another said, "I will surround it with a wall of fire."

D. A third said, "I will surround it with a wall of iron."

E. Said the Holy One, blessed be he, "Do you take pride in what belongs to me? By your life, I shall show you that you are nothing."

F. What did he do?

G. He went and changed the names of the angels, so that the angel who ruled water was made to rule over fire, and the one who ruled fire was to rule iron, and when below they called on these names, the ones above did not respond: "he has brought down to the ground in dishonor the kingdom and its rulers."

H. When on account of their sins, the enemy came, and the people called on a given angel, "Come and do thus and so for us," he answered, "I don't have the power, since I have been removed from that element."

5. A. Another interpretation of the verse, "he has brought down to the ground in dishonor the kingdom and its rulers":

B. "the kingdom": this is Zedekiah, king of Judah.

C. "and its rulers": this is the rulers above.

The exegesis is now systematic and works clause by clause, under-lining the odd character of the foregoing. Nos. 2 and 3 serve as a prologue for No. 4, or all three form a coherent whole.

9

Parashah II
Lamentations 2:3

He has cut down in fierce anger all the might of Israel;
he has withdrawn from them his right hand
in the face of the enemy;
he has burned like a flaming fire in Jacob,
consuming all around.

One recurrent interest of our sages is to link all moments in the sacred history of Israel to each event. In our reading of the base verse at hand, we see how sages find it possible to invoke all occasions in the reading of one event.

LIX.i.
1. A. "He has cut down in fierce anger all the might [horn] of Israel":
   B. There are ten references to "might" [horn] of Israel: Abraham, Isaac, Joseph, Moses, the Torah, the priesthood, the Levites, prophecy, the Temple, and Israel.

C. Some add, "The might [horn] of the Messiah."

D. "Abraham": "My well-beloved had a vineyard in a very fruitful hill" (Is. 5:1). [The reference is to the ram sacrificed in place of Isaac (Cohen, p. 168, n. 3).]

E. "Isaac": "Caught in the thicket by his horns" (Gen. 22: 13).

F. "Joseph": "And his horns are the horns of the wild ox" (Dt. 33:17).

G. "Moses": "The skin of his face sent forth beams" (Ex. 34:29).

H. "the Torah": "Horns he has from his hands" (Hab. 3:4).

I. "the priesthood": "His horn shall be exalted in honor" (Ps. 112:9).

J. "the Levites": "All these were the sons of Heman the king's seer in the things pertaining to God to lift up the horn" (1 Chr. 24:5).

K. "prophecy": "My horn is exalted in the Lord" (1 Sam. 2:1).

L. "the Temple": "From the horns of the wild oxen do you answer me" (Ps. 22:22).

M. "and Israel": "And he has lifted up a horn for his people" (Ps. 148:14).

N. Some add, "The might [horn] of the Messiah": "And he will give strength to his king and exalt the horn of his anointed" (1 Sam. 2:10).

O. All of them were set on the head of Israel, but when the Israelites sinned, they were taken away from them and given to the nations of the world: "He has cut down in fierce anger all the might [horn] of Israel."

P. So it is said, "And concerning the ten horns that were on its head and the other horn which came up and before which three fell. . . . And so for the ten horns out of this kingdom shall ten kings arise; and another shall arise after them; and he shall be different from the former, and he shall put down three kings" (Dan. 7:20, 24).

Q. But when the Israelites repent, the Holy One, blessed be he, will put the horns back in place: "All the horns of the wicked I will also cut off, but the horns of the righteous shall be lifted up" (Ps. 75:11).

R. The horns which the Righteous One of the world had cut off [will be restored].

S. When will he restore them to their place?

T. When the Holy One, blessed be he, exalts the horn of his messiah: "And he will give strength to his king and exalt the horn of his anointed" (1 Sam. 2:10).

This is a fine and well-composed composition, which vastly expands the framework in which we read the book of Lamentations and underlines the lesson to be learned: when the Israelites repent, the Holy One, blessed be he, will put the horns back in place: "All the horns of the wicked I will also cut off, but the horns of the righteous shall be lifted up" (Ps. 75:11). That message obviously is not particular to our book, but it does belong in the setting of the occasion for mourning on which our book is read in the synagogue.

LIX:ii.

1. A. "he has withdrawn from them his right hand in the face of the enemy":

B. R. Azariah in the name of R. Judah b. R. Simon: "When by reason of sin the enemy entered the sanctuary, they seized the warriors and tied their hands behind their back.

C. "Said the Holy One, blessed be he, 'I have already taken an oath to my children, "I will be with him in trouble" (Ps. 91:15).

D. "'Now that my children are distressed while I am at ease — if one could say it — "he has withdrawn from them his right hand."'

E. "In the end he revealed it to Daniel: 'But do you wait till the end be' (Dan. 12:13).

F. "He said to him, 'What end?'

G. "He said to him, 'To give judgment and a final accounting.'

H. "He said to him, 'And you shall rest.'

I. "He said to him, 'Is it to be forever?'

J. "He said to him, 'And you shall arise.'

K. "He said to him, 'With whom, the righteous or the wicked?'

L. "He said to him, 'To your lot,' meaning, with the righteous.'

M. "He said to him, 'Will this come in the end of days or in the end of the right hand?'

N. "He said to him, 'At the end of the right hand, the right hand that has become enslaved. I have set an end for my right hand, when I redeemed my children, I shall redeem my right hand too.'

O. "That is in line with this verse: 'That your beloved ones may be delivered, save your right hand and answer me' (Ps. 60:7)."

The familiar theme of God's engagement with the disaster of Israel is expressed in a fresh way. The exposition of the base verse, "he has withdrawn from them his right hand," allows the point to be made that God did not abandon Israel but suffered with them. Daniel 12:13 then works as an intersecting verse, even though in form the composition does not conform to the anticipated pattern.

LIX:iii.

1. A. "he has burned like a flaming fire in Jacob, consuming all around":

B. Said R. Simeon b. Laqish, "When the punishment comes to the world, only Jacob feels it first of all: 'he has burned like a flaming fire in Jacob.'

C. "But when joy comes to the world, only Jacob feels it first of all: 'Let Jacob rejoice, let Israel be glad' (Ps. 14:7)."

The match of punishment and restoration or healing is made once again; Israel is first to suffer, first to rejoice. So the unfortunate condition of Israel underlines the conviction that Israel stands at the center of things.

10

Parashah III
Lamentations 3:16–18

He has made my teeth grind on gravel
and made me cower in ashes;
my soul is bereft of peace,
I have forgotten what happiness is;
so I say, "Gone is my glory,
and my expectation from the Lord."

Once more we move from exegesis of verses to narratives regarded as illustrative of the sense of verses. The story that is told is a biting one.

LXXXIV.i.

1. A. "He has made my teeth grind on gravel and made me cower in ashes":

   B. There is the case of the son of R. Hanina b. Teradion, who joined up with guerillas. He snitched on them and they killed him.

C. His father went and found him in the wilderness, with his mouth full of dirt and gravel.

D. A few days later they put him in a coffin and out of respect for his father, they wanted to have a eulogy said for him. The father would not permit it. He said to them, "Let me speak concerning my son."

E. He commenced by citing this verse: "Neither have I hearkened to the voice of my teachers, nor inclined my ear to those who taught me. I was well nigh in all evil in the midst of the congregation and assembly" (Prov. 5:13–14).

F. His mother commenced by citing this verse over him: "A foolish son is a vexation to his father, and bitterness to her that bore him" (Prov. 17:25).

G. His sister cited this verse: "Bread of falsehood is sweet to a man, but afterwards his mouth will be filled with gravel" (Prov. 20:17).

A trait of our sages — and of the Judaism that they formed — is their blunt and unapologetic directness. They do not circumlocute, and they do not "spiritualize" or smooth off rough messages. The boy was a snitch, so the ones who killed him stuffed dirt in his mouth, in the manner of the time and place. All three who spoke dirges, father, mother, and sister, acknowledged the facts of the case — no pretense, no deception, no disingenuous apologetics.

The next reading of our base verse is equally out of phase with the requirements of a systematic commentary. To the base verse we add a rule of law on conduct on the ninth of Ab, together with an illustration of the rule; the connection to the base verse is then clear.

2. A. "He has made my teeth grind on gravel and made me cower in ashes":

B. We have learned: On the eve of the ninth of Ab, one may not eat meat nor drink wine nor may one cook two cooked dishes, nor may one bathe and anoint the body. But at a meal not prior to the fast of the ninth of Ab [on the eighth of Ab, that is] one may eat meat, drink wine, and enjoy two cooked dishes.

C. When Rab would eat the meal prior to the ninth of Ab,
he took a piece of bread, sprinkled some ashes on it, and
said, "This is the meal prior to the ninth of Ab, meant to
fulfill this verse: 'He has made my teeth grind on gravel
and made me cower in ashes.'"

The base verse is now illustrated with stories that underline
its main point: Israel has forgotten the meaning of happiness, or
luxury, or comfort.

3. A. "my soul is bereft of peace, I have forgotten what happiness is":
   B. Said R. Eleazar b. R. Yosé in the name of R. Hananiah b.
R. Abbahu, "There is the case of a woman in Caesarea,
who took her son to a baker and said to him, 'Teach my
son the trade.'
   C. "He said to her, 'Leave him with me for five years, and I
shall teach him how to make five hundred kinds of wheat
bread.'"
   D. R. Aha and Rabbis:
   E. R. Aha said, "With wheat of *minnit* [Ez. 27:17] there is
no limit to the kinds of bread one can make."
   F. Rabbis said, "There are five hundred kinds of bread that
one can make with wheat, according to the numerical
value of the letters of the word *minnit*."
   G. R. Hinena and R. Jonathan were in session and counted
up to sixty before concluding.
4. A. [A further illustration of the verse, "my soul is bereft of
peace, I have forgotten what happiness is":]
   B. Said R. Eleazar b. R. Yosé, "There was the case of a
woman who brought her son to a cook and said to him,
'Teach my son the trade.'
   C. "He said to her, 'Leave him with me for five years, and
I shall teach him how to make five hundred kinds of
omelettes.'"
   D. Rabbi [Judah the Patriarch] heard and said, "That kind of
luxury we have never seen" [after the destruction of the

Temple, thus "my soul is bereft of peace, I have forgotten what happiness is"].

E. R. Simeon b. Halafta heard and said, "Of such luxury we have never even heard."

5. A. [A further illustration of the verse, "my soul is bereft of peace, I have forgotten what happiness is":] R. Judah b. Betera came to Nisibis on the eve of the great fast [the Day of Atonement].

B. He ate and finished [eating prior to the fast].

C. The head of the community came to him to invite him. He said to him, "I have already eaten and completed eating [prior to the fast]."

D. He said to him, "Pay attention to me, [Cohen: 'Let my master favor me by coming to my house for the meal'], so that people should not say that that master paid no attention to me."

E. Since he insisted, the other went with him.

F. The head of the community [Cohen, p. 197:] thereupon instructed his young servant, saying, "Any course which you serve us once must not be repeated."

G. They brought before them eighty courses, and he took a small taste of each, and drank a cup of each jar of wine.

H. The host said to him, "My lord, did you not say to me, 'I have already eaten and finished [the final meal prior to the Day of Atonement]'? Now you were served with eighty courses, and you took a small taste of each, and drank a cup of each jar of wine. [Cohen, p. 197, n. 3: He made this remark to boast of his lavish hospitality and insinuate that his guest had previously had an insufficient meal.]

I. He said to him, "Why is it that the appetite is called capacious [nefesh]? The more you give it, the more it expands [nefishah]."

6. A. [A further illustration of the verse, "my soul is bereft of peace, I have forgotten what happiness is":] R. Abbahu went to Bosrah and was received by Yosé, nicknamed "the head."

B. They brought before him eighty kinds of birds' brains.

C. He said to him, "Let my lord not be angry with me, for the yield [of birds today] has not been enough."

D. People called him "the head" because all his food was only birds' brains.

7. A. [A further illustration of the verse, "my soul is bereft of peace, I have forgotten what happiness is":] R. Hiyya the Elder went to the South and was received by R. Joshua b. Levi.

B. Twenty-four cooked dishes were set before him.

C. He said to him, "What do you do then on the Sabbath [which is marked by more substantial meals than the weekday]?"

D. He said to him, "We have double that number."

E. Later on R. Joshua b. Levi went to Tiberias and was received by R. Hiyya the Elder.

F. The host gave the disciples of R. Joshua some funds and said to them, "Go, buy for your master what he is used to eating."

8. A. [A further illustration of the verse, "my soul is bereft of peace, I have forgotten what happiness is":] R. Isaac b. R. Eliezer knew the proper sequence of meals in accord with the days of the year [so that on each day he would serve a different menu].

B. That is when he could afford it.

C. But when he could not afford it, he would take fruit pits and count them in order not to forget them.

9. A. "I have forgotten what happiness is":

B. Taught R. Simeon b. Gamaliel, "This refers to washing the hands and feet after a bath."

10. A. "so I say, 'Gone is my glory, and my expectation from the Lord'":

B. Said R. Simeon b. Laqish, "Even though the Holy One, blessed be he, grows angry with his servants, the righteous, in this world, he goes and has mercy upon them:

C. "That is in line with this verse: 'so I say, "Gone is my glory, and my expectation from the Lord."'" [Cohen, p. 198, n. 7, interprets the sense as follows: "so I say, 'Gone is my glory' " — in this world, but "and my expectation from the Lord — in the world to come."]

No. 1 has no bearing upon the interpretation of our document. The pertinence clearly derives from the reference to "making teeth grind on gravel," but even the texts cited by the members of the deceased's family do not allude to our base verse. No. 2 is relevant in a general way; at least the base verse serves as a proof text. Nos. 3–7 illustrate the level of luxury that prevailed.

11

Israel and History: From Events to Rules

A variety of messages have passed before us, and yet if among them I had to select one point that unites every passage, it is that Israel is responsible for its own condition but also can so act as to atone for what it has done and so regain God's favor. A covenant governs Israel's relationship to God, and therefore the condition of the holy people. When the covenant is broken, the result is God's punishment; but then, when Israel atones, the covenant makes clear, Israel will repair its disastrous condition. That is to say, our compilers have focused upon a single message, the one beginning with Deuteronomy.

Theirs is a covenantal theology, in which Israel and God have mutually and reciprocally agreed to bind themselves to a common Torah; the rules of the relationship are such that an infraction triggers its penalty willy-nilly; but obedience to the Torah likewise brings its reward, in the context envisaged by our compilers, the reward of redemption. Our survey has uncovered the fact, amazing to me, that there are no varieties of messages but only one message, and it is reworked in only a few ways: Israel suffers because of sin, but God will respond to Israel's atonement, on the one side, and loyalty to the covenant in the Torah, on the other. And when Israel has attained the merit that accrues through the Torah, God will redeem Israel. That is the simple, rock-hard, and repeated message of this rather protracted reading of the book of Lamentations. Whether it is also the message of Lamentations (and, along with Lamentations, Jeremiah, and, in the same context, Deuteronomy, Joshua, Judges, Samuel, and Kings, not to mention the rest of the Torah) is not relevant here.

We began with the observation that through scripture the sages accomplished their writing, and we have further noted throughout that it is not so much by writing fresh discourses as by compiling and arranging materials that the framers of the document accomplished that writing. It would be difficult to find a less promising mode of writing than merely collecting and arranging available compositions and turning them into a composite. But that in the aggregate is the predominant trait of this writing. That our compilers were interested in the exposition of the book of Lamentations equally as much as in the execution of their paramount proposition through their compilation is clear. For we have a large number of entries that contain no more elaborate proposition than the exposition through paraphrase of the sense of a given clause or verse.

Indeed, Lamentations Rabbah proves nearly as much a commentary in the narrowest sense — verse-by-verse amplification, paraphrase, exposition — as it is a compilation in the working definition of this inquiry of mine. What holds the document together and gives it, if not coherence, then at least flow and movement, after all, are the successive passages of (mere) exposition. The important collection of stories that the compilation includes vastly expands the definition of "mere exposition," to be sure. But the whole does hang together. For it is stunning to realize the simple fact that, when all has been set forth and completed, there really is that simple message that God's relationship with Israel, which is unique among the nations, works itself out even now, in a time of despair and disappointment. The resentment of the present condition, recapitulating the calamity of the destruction of the Temple, finds its resolution and remission in the redemption that will follow Israel's regeneration through the Torah — that is the program, that is the proposition, and in this compilation, there is no other. What that now-demonstrated fact of description of the compilation means is simple. Our authorship decided to compose a document concerning the book of Lamentations in order to make a single point. Everything else was subordinated to that definitive intention. Once the work got underway, the task was one not so much of exposition as of repetition, not unpacking and exploring a complex conception, but restating the point on the one side and eliciting or evoking the proper attitude that was congruent with that point on the other. The decision, viewed after the fact, was to make one statement in an enormous number of ways. This highly restricted program of thought resorted to a singularly varied vocabulary. Indeed, some might call it a symbolic vocabulary, in that messages are conveyed not through propositions, but through images, whether visual or verbal.

As they responded to it, scripture supplied a highly restricted vocabulary. The message was singular; the meanings were few and to be repeated, not many to be cast aside promiscuously. When we find the sequences proposing "another interpretation," we see how this works: a great many ways are found to say one thing. That is why we do not find endless multiple meanings[1] but a highly limited repertoire of a few cogent and wholly coherent meanings, to be replayed again and again. It is the repetitious character of discourse, in which people say the same thing in a great many different ways, that characterizes this document. The treatment of the Lamentations by our sages of blessed memory who compiled Lamentations Rabbah shows over and over again that long lists of alternative meanings or interpretations end up saying just one thing, but in different ways. The implicit meanings prove very few indeed.

So through propositional discourse on the one side and through narrative on the other — the one aiming at the intellect, the other at the emotions — our compilers, who really constituted an authorship, a single, single-minded, and determined group (whether of one or ten or two hundred workers hardly matters), set forth their variation on a very old and profoundly rooted theology. What was new to them was not the message, but the medium. It was one thing to write with scripture; that had been done before. It was quite another to write by collecting and arranging verses of scripture in such a way that many things were made to say one thing. In Lamentations Rabbah, many things do say one thing, and here, we see, God lives not only in the details, but in the repetition of details, always in the same way, always with the same message — quite another meaning implicit in God's unity.

To say that "God lives in the repetition of the details" is a theological way of saying that there are rules that govern the destiny of the social entity, Israel, and the working of these rules plays itself out in things that happen to Israel, which is to say, in events, or in what we call in abstract language "history." It follows that the composition of singular events into exemplary cases, the transformation of this and that ("one damn thing after another") into history — these form the program of our document, as they do a variety of other documents in the Judaism of the dual Torah in its final formulation. When people contemplated the past, it was because they proposed through such precise knowledge to explain whatever mattered in the present. History therefore defined a principal medium of discourse about the shape and structure of culture, explaining, classifying, evaluating. Many times in our survey of Leviticus Rabbah we have seen examples of that fact. What people chose to interpret in the present then defined their curiosity about the past. They then identified out of the unlimited agenda of the past those things that mattered, and these they called events, occasions of consequence, as distinct from undifferentiated and unperceived happenings — from eating breakfast to losing one's keys — which of course bear no material consequence in the explanation of the world.

We now understand that the very notion of an "event," and with it the vast superstructure of the ordering of intellect and the explanation of society built upon the historical explanation of sequences of happenings identified as consequential, thus, as events (then to now, there to here, all rational, all obvious, all self-evident) — these come to us as the gifts of naive credulity. It follows that the definition of events — the destruction of the Temple for our authorship, the death of a single human being for other writers of the same age — forms an acutely concrete statement of the larger systemic principles, and when we understand how a system defines events, we grasp the working of that system.

Let me offer as my initial instance not Judaism, but a different matter altogether, one that gives us perspective on the question I mean to approach as my case: What, in Judaism, is an event, and how, from Judaism, do we learn about the hermeneutics of events? And what exactly does Judaism mean by "events"? To find the answer to that question succinctly is simple. When we know how Judaism *classifies* events, we shall have the answer to the question of defining events — a perfectly routine procedure in the natural history of ideas. So too, when we know how Judaism *utilizes* events, assessing with accuracy and on the basis of a vast and characteristic kind of writing the heuristic value, the probative standing, of events, we once again shall have our answer. And in the document before us, we have seen a rich and textured account of our answer.

In the canonical literature of the Judaism of the dual Torah, events find their place within the science of learning, of *Listenwissenschaft* that characterizes this literature, along with the sorts of things that for our part we should not characterize as events at all. It follows that the Judaism of the canon in no way appeals to history as a sequence of ordered events, yielding a clear truth and meaning in the way, for instance, that history in the Deuteronomic sequence of Deuteronomy, Joshua, Judges, Samuel, and Kings forms a sequence of events that comprise history. In canonical Judaism, by contrast, events have no autonomous standing; events are not unique, each unto itself; events have no probative value on their own; and events are not to be strung together as explanations for how things are. In this writing — which is philosophical and scientific, rather than historical and theological — events form cases. Then, formed into lists of things, they in common point to, or prove, one thing.

Not only so, but events do not make up their own list at all, and this is what I found rather curious when I first noted that fact. That is to say, just as in the canon of Judaism of the dual Torah there is not a single piece of writing of sustained narrative, something we might call history, as Josephus or the Deuteronomists wrote history,

so we have only episodically and then unsustainedly the representation of events as merely exemplary, never probative by reason of
connection and sequence and order. Events therefore do not form
components of an independent variable, and history constitutes no
independent variable. Events will appear on — form components
of — the same list as persons, places, things. That means that events
not only have no autonomous standing on their own, but also that
events constitute no species even within a genus, the historical order.
For persons, places, and things in our way of thinking do not belong
on the same list as events; they are not of the same order.

A happening is no different from an object, in which case "event"
serves no better, and no worse, than a hero, a gesture or action, a
recitation of a given formula, or a particular locale to establish a
truth. It is contingent, subordinate, instrumental. As our document
has shown us, an event is not at all eventful; it is merely a fact that
forms part of the evidence for what is. And what is eventful is not
an occasion at all, but a condition, an attitude, a perspective, and a
viewpoint. Then, it is clear, events are subordinated to the formation
of attitudes, perspectives, viewpoints — the formative artifacts not
of history in the conventional sense, but of culture. List-making —
whether lists of events or persons or types of toothpick, for that
matter — is accomplished within a restricted repertoire of items that
can serve on lists; the list-making then presents interesting combina-
tions of an essentially small number of candidates for the exercise.
But then when making lists, one can do pretty much anything with
the items that are combined; the taxic indicators are unlimited, but
the data studied are severely limited. And that fact returns us to our
starting point, the observations on history as a cultural artifact that
form the premise for the study of history within the archaeology of
knowledge. In fact, in Judaism history serves the theological sciences
and therefore cannot be said to constitute history in any ordinary
sense at all; but that is a trivial and obvious observation. More to
the point, history, in the form of events, contributes to a rather odd
way of conducting theological science.

History constitutes one among a variety of what I call, for lack of
more suitable language at this point, theological "things" — names,
places, events, actions deemed to bear theological weight and to

affect attitude and action. When three or more such theological "things" — whether person, event, action, or attitude — are combined, they form a theological structure, and, viewed all together, all of the theological "things" in a given document constitute the components of the entire theological structure that the document affords. The upshot is that in an exact sense, "event" or "history" standing by itself has no meaning at all in Judaism, since Judaism forms culture through other than historical modes of organizing existence. Without the social construction of history, there also is no need for the identification of events, that is, individual and unique happenings that bear consequence, since, within the system and structure of Judaism, history forms no taxon, assuredly not the paramount one. It must follow, then, that no happening is unique, and no event, on its own, bears consequence.

These statements rest upon modes of the analysis of history as the fabrication of culture, including a religious culture, and require us to review the recent formation of thought on history as culturally ordered and on the event as "contingent realization of the cultural pattern." It is only in that context that we may make sense, also, of the representation of both history and its raw materials, events, in Judaism in its definitive canon. That is the lesson to be learned from Lamentations Rabbah.

The importance of that lesson becomes clear in light of a recent decision by authorities of Judaism all over the world. When, after World War II, the sages of Judaism had to respond to the unparalleled catastrophe of the years from 1933 through 1945, many naturally assumed that the ninth of Ab (generally in early August) would mark the day of mourning, and the reading of the book of Lamentations, the correct liturgy. But that is not what happened. Rather, a distinct occasion, "the day of the Holocaust," was designated, separate from the ninth of Ab. In the early years after World War II, the word that was often used to describe what had happened was *hurban,* the word that is used to speak of the destruction of the first Temple and of the second Temple (and much else). But the word that later came to be used for those events was a different one, namely, *shoah,* translated into English as "Holocaust." So at both points, a consensus took shape that the calamity of the twentieth century was not to be subsumed under the rubric of *hurban* on the ninth of Ab.

The reason for that decision was articulated: what had happened was unique, without antecedent or parallel, and hence a singular word and a particular commemoration were required. Judaism had been so changed by those events that its inherited responses, the rites and rituals that had served through centuries of calamities, no longer served. Israel, the holy people, could no longer subsume events within known rules; a new event had taken place that violated all of the rules, and that had to be treated as not exemplary but distinctive, not a case of a general condition but a unique and singular case. That accounts for the general observance in contemporary Judaism of two distinct days of mourning: the ninth of Ab for all times and places of disaster, and Holocaust-day for that unique calamity unto itself.

I am inclined to think that our sages, who gave us Lamentations Rabbah, would have dissented from that decision. They found ample reason to imagine that the events of the destruction of the second Temple, or the catastrophe of the defeat of Bar Kokhba, had no parallel, fell under no rule, fit with no prior classification. But they took the opposite view: God rules, always and in the same way. The covenant of Sinai endures, governing all that happens — and explaining everything. These are profound questions, matters on which honorable people will disagree for a long time to come.

Note

1. Cf. William Scott Green, "Romancing the Tome: Rabbinic Hermeneutics and the Theory of Literature," *Semeia* 40 (1987):147–69, with special reference to p. 163: "If it is doubtful that rabbis ascribed 'endless multiple meanings' to scripture, it is no less so that rabbinic hermeneutics encouraged and routinely tolerated the metonymical coexistence of different meanings of scripture that did not, and could not, annul one another."

Index